POWER
PRAYERS

to

Grow Your Faith

POWER PRAYERS

to

Grow Your Faith

VALUEBOOKS

An Imprint of Barbour Publishing, Inc.

© 2014 by Barbour Publishing

Print ISBN 978-1-62836-641-9

eBook Editions:
Adobe Digital Edition (.epub) 978-1-63058-071-1
Kindle and MobiPocket Edition (.prc) 978-1-63058-072-8

Text compiled from *Power Prayers for Grads*, *Power Prayers for Mothers*, *Power Prayers for Men*, and *Power Prayers to Start Your Day*.

All scripture quotations, unless otherwise noted, are taken from the King James Version of the Bible.

Scripture quotations marked NKJV are taken from the New King James Version®. Copyright © 1982 by Thomas Nelson, Inc. Used by permission. All rights reserved.

Scripture quotations marked NIV are taken from the HOLY BIBLE, NEW INTERNATIONAL VERSION®. NIV®. Copyright © 1973, 1978, 1984, 2011 by Biblica, Inc.™ Used by permission. All rights reserved worldwide.

Scripture quotations marked MSG are from *THE MESSAGE*. Copyright © by Eugene H. Peterson 1993, 1994, 1995, 1996, 2000, 2001, 2002. Used by permission of NavPress Publishing Group.

Scripture quotations marked ESV are from The Holy Bible, English Standard Version®, copyright © 2001 by Crossway Bibles, a publishing ministry of Good News Publishers. Used by permission. All rights reserved.

Scripture quotations marked NLT are taken from the *Holy Bible*. New Living Translation copyright© 1996, 2004, 2007 by Tyndale House Foundation. Used by permission of Tyndale House Publishers. Carol Stream, Illinois 60188. All rights reserved.

Scripture quotations marked NASB are taken from the New American Standard Bible, © 1960, 1962, 1963, 1968, 1971, 1972, 1973, 1975, 1977, 1995 by The Lockman Foundation. Used by permission.

Scripture quotations marked AMP are taken from the Amplified® Bible, © 1954, 1958, 1962, 1964, 1965, 1987 by The Lockman Foundation. Used by permission.

Scripture quotations marked NCV are taken from the New Century Version of the Bible, copyright © 2005 by Thomas Nelson, Inc. Used by permission. All rights reserved.

Published by Barbour Publishing, Inc., P.O. Box 719, Uhrichsville, Ohio 44683,
www.barbourbooks.com

Our mission is to publish and distribute inspirational products offering exceptional value and biblical encouragement to the masses.

Evangelical Christian
Publishers Association

Printed in the United States of America.

Contents

Introduction

∞

The Power of Prayer

Faith! What a small word with enormous implications. Hebrews 11:1 describes faith as "confidence in what we hope for and assurance about what we do not see" (NIV). When the disciples asked Jesus to increase their faith, Christ assured them that they needed only the faith of a mustard seed. In a glorious display of spiritual hyperbole, Christ explained that faith the size of a mustard seed could move mountains. And though we do not see mountains being flung around as the result of our faith, we have certainly witnessed what God can do when we put our confidence in Him. Lives can be changed and hearts can be softened—mountain-moving work. No doubt even the tiniest bit of faith goes a long way.

Perhaps one of the kindest things Christ requested of His followers was this faith the size of a mustard seed, meaning faith is not only essential for the Christian walk, it is attainable. While Christ could have requested faith the size of planets or of oceans—certainly He had a right to do so as the Son of God—He instead insisted that His people trust Him with faith that equates to seeds only one or two millimeters in size. By requiring a faith this small,

Christ acknowledged our frailty as human beings and assured His people that what they lacked, God could more than supply.

Thomas Watson, a puritan preacher from the 17th century said: "The promise is not made to strong faith, but to true. The promise doth not say, Whosoever hath a giant faith that can remove mountains, that can stop the mouth of lions, shall be saved; but whosoever believes, be his faith never so small."

Faith is necessary for all of life—for salvation, growth, daily living, prayer, provision, and death. For the believer, it is the air we breathe.

In the perfect wisdom of God, He takes our faith—small and pitiful though it is at times—and He plants it in the garden of His goodness and waters it with our prayers so that when it comes to fruition, nothing is impossible for us. When God's children kneel before their maker, believing that God can do what He says He can do and claiming the promises of the Bible, God's inexhaustible capacity to accomplish good is unleashed on those with true faith! What unfathomable kindness!

✦ *How to Use This Book* ✦

Power Prayers to Grow Your Faith is a guide to help you develop a more faith-filled walk with your heavenly Father in every area of your life. It is divided into chapters according to topics relevant to life and faith, such as forgiveness, compassion, and fellowship. Read them in order or start with the topic of your choice.

Many prayers include a scripture referenece. Feel free to pray God's Word back to Him. God's own words carry with them the confidence that He will hear and bless. Read and apply the scriptures. Allow the prayers to become your own. Keep a pen and notebook handy to record your own thoughts and prayers or write your thoughts in the margins of this book. When appropriate, you might share selections with your family so that they, too, can grow in their faith.

I fervently hope you will more fully experience your growing faith as you read these selections. May God bless you in this endeavor!

"For truly, I say to you, if you have faith like a grain of mustard seed, you will say to this mountain, 'Move from here to there,' and it will move, and nothing will be impossible for you."
MATTHEW 17:20 ESV

CHAPTER 1

My Salvation: The Power of Unconditional Love

❧

God established His plan of salvation even before the world began. He knew we would sin, and He created us anyway. Revelation 13:8 calls Jesus "the Lamb slain from the foundation of the world" Jesus knew He would be the sacrifice who would pay for our sins. He understood He would leave the glory of heaven and take up residence in this evil-infested world. He was prepared to be rejected by many whom He loved. By far, the worst thing He would endure would be His Father's rejection as He was covered with our sins. Yes, Christ knew before creation what part He would play. It was horrible but necessary, and He was willing.

Why then do so many reject Him or try to get to heaven on their own merit? Christ did all that needs to be done. Our part is simply to accept Him. Certainly He will begin to change us once we trust Him as our Savior, but that is a result of salvation, not the cause of it.

Matthew 18:3 says, "Verily I say unto you, Except ye be converted, and become as little children, ye shall not enter into the kingdom of heaven."

What a blessing it is to see a child bow before the God of the universe and to trust Him as Savior! But it is equally thrilling when an adult becomes as trusting as a child and seeks God's forgiveness. Ardell was eighty-two when she found Jesus. Although she had taught Sunday school, she didn't truly know the salvation of the Lord. What a difference it made when she accepted Him.

What is your position with Jesus? Do you know Him as Savior, or are you trying to be righteous on your own? Do you understand how offensive your sin is to our holy God? Romans 3:10 says, "There is none righteous, no, not one." All of us are sinners, and because of this we deserve death—eternal punishment in hell. "For the wages of sin is death; but the gift of God is eternal life through Jesus Christ our Lord" (Romans 6:23).

Did you notice the word *but*? Yes, we deserve death, *but* God loved us so much that even before He made us, He established a plan to save us. Still, salvation is not automatic. Our part is to call on Christ (see Romans 10:10).

If you have committed your life to Christ, rejoice! You have the greatest of blessings. If you've never trusted Christ, won't you do it today? If you reject Him, nothing else in this book matters. Having a clean heart before God and helping those around you to have the same are the greatest gifts imaginable. Carefully consider that as you read the following passages.

❧ White as Snow ❦

Come now, and let us reason together, saith the LORD:
though your sins be as scarlet, they shall be as white as snow;
though they be red like crimson, they shall be as wool.
ISAIAH 1:18

My children love snow so much they've requested
it as early as September. Father, You know how I
chuckled about that. You know how we considered
praying that it would hold off until Christmas. Yet
when it came to our children having their hearts
washed "white as snow," we were eager to see it
happen. It became a time of rejoicing for all of us.

❧ Don't Let the Little Ones Perish ❦

Even so it is not the will of your Father which is in
heaven, that one of these little ones should perish.
MATTHEW 18:14

Lord, I'm so glad You often used children in Your
teachings and emphasized the importance of bring-
ing them to You. Otherwise we might fail to share
Your salvation with them. I remember how excited
I was as a small child when I gave my life to You.
When my children recognized Your salvation was
for them, my heart sang. What a precious gift—
Your love for children.

❖ Saved through Christ Alone ❖

Neither is there salvation in any other: for there is none other name under heaven given among men, whereby we must be saved.

ACTS 4:12

Lord Jesus, how sad You must be when You see the pride that consumes humanity. The gift of salvation was a great sacrifice for You, but now it is readily available to us. Yet so many people try to save themselves. Some call on You for their salvation but trust in themselves to work out the details. Others live only for the moment and refuse to acknowledge their need. I'm so glad You saved me, Lord. Thank You for eternal life!

❖ A Prayer of Christ ❖

Father, the hour is come; glorify thy Son, that thy Son also may glorify thee: as thou hast given him power over all flesh, that he should give eternal life to as many as thou hast given him. And this is life eternal, that they might know thee the only true God, and Jesus Christ, whom thou hast sent. I have glorified thee on the earth: I have finished the work which thou gavest me to do.

JOHN 17:1–4

❧ Belief, Confession, Salvation ☙

*If thou shalt confess with thy mouth the Lord Jesus,
and shalt believe in thine heart that God hath raised
him from the dead, thou shalt be saved. For with the
heart man believeth unto righteousness; and with the
mouth confession is made unto salvation.*
ROMANS 10:9–10

Lord, when I look at what You're saying about how
I can be saved, I'm amazed. Father, prepare more
hearts to believe in Jesus. Let more people confess
that You alone can save. Grow my faith!

❧ Saved for Christ's Purpose ☙

*[God] hath saved us, and called us with an holy
calling, not according to our works, but according
to his own purpose and grace, which was given
us in Christ Jesus before the world began.*
2 TIMOTHY 1:9

Oh great God, before You spoke this world into
existence, You had me in mind. You knew I would
fail and need cleansing, and You had a plan. You
gave Your Son to pay the price for my sin. I cannot
fathom the depth of Your love. I can't imagine sac-
rificing a child, but You did. How passionate Your
love is!

✦ Seek Christ Now ✦

*Seek ye the LORD while he may be found,
call ye upon him while he is near.*

ISAIAH 55:6

How You long to save the lost and dying, Lord Jesus! How eager You are to cleanse us from our sins. From the sweet voices of tiny children to the final breaths of elderly grandparents, the plea for forgiveness and salvation fills You with delight. Oh Father, may many more people seek You while You may be found.

✦ Seeing Salvation ✦

*And he came by the Spirit into the temple: and when
the parents brought in the child Jesus, to do for him
after the custom of the law, then took he him up in
his arms, and blessed God, and said, Lord, now lettest
thou thy servant depart in peace, according to thy
word: for mine eyes have seen thy salvation.*

LUKE 2:27–30

✢ Christ Can Save ✦

Wherefore he is able also to save them to the uttermost that come unto God by him, seeing he ever liveth to make intercession for them.

HEBREWS 7:25

I've known a lot of bad people, Jesus. Although I must not embrace their lifestyles, I can show them Your love. It isn't my place to decide who is worthy of Your grace. I must share You with everyone I meet. Help me to be an example to those around me of the truth that Your salvation is for all who come to You.

✢ In a Looking Glass ✦

But we all, with open face beholding as in a glass the glory of the Lord, are changed into the same image from glory to glory, even as by the Spirit of the Lord.

2 CORINTHIANS 3:18

You are changing me, Lord, and I'm glad. The more I see You, the more I become like You. It's a work You began when You agreed to go to the cross for my sins. To be identified with You is the utmost privilege. Oh, what a glorious day is coming when I become like You; for I will see You as You are!

✦ Work It Out ✦

Wherefore, my beloved, as ye have always obeyed,
not as in my presence only, but now much more
in my absence, work out your own salvation
with fear and trembling.
PHILIPPIANS 2:12

Almighty God, Your salvation ensures I will spend eternity with You rather than in hell, but it means so much more than that. I am saved to bring glory to Your name and enjoy Your presence. You have a plan for me now that You've given this marvelous gift. I must honor and live for You. I must bring others to You.

✦ Taking Up My Cross ✦

And he said to them all, If any man will
come after me, let him deny himself,
and take up his cross daily,
and follow me.
LUKE 9:23

You have given me eternal life, Jesus, and no one can take it from me. There's nothing I can do that will make me more or less saved. Still, I will live for You.

So many people don't understand this commitment. I want to be identified with You, though, precious Savior, and if that requires being misunderstood, mocked, or even persecuted, I am willing.

⇨ *You Brought Me Out of Bondage* ⇦

And thou shalt shew thy son in that day, saying,
This is done because of that which the LORD *did*
unto me when I came forth out of Egypt.
EXODUS 13:8

Great Deliverer, I was enslaved in the worst way. Sin held me captive, and I could not break free, but in Your grace and mercy You freed me. I want to be a living testament to the victory You won in my soul.

My family needs to see this. They need to understand the bondage of sin and the freedom they can have in You. My testimony will draw my loved ones to You.

→ False Zeal ←

For I bear them record that they have a zeal of God,
but not according to knowledge.
ROMANS 10:2

Dear God, there are many religious people who know there has to be a higher being, but that's the only understanding they have. They are afraid they will offend this "god," so they make up a religion to avoid it. Some people are relying on religious beliefs that have no scriptural backing. Help me to share Your truth so more people will be saved.

CHAPTER 2

My Bible: The Power of the Living Word

∞

And he came to Nazareth, where he had been brought up: and, as his custom was, he went into the synagogue on the sabbath day, and stood up for to read.

LUKE 4:16

Jesus, the living Word of God, loved sharing scripture with those He came to save. He understood the powerful influence the Bible would have on their lives if they willingly received it.

We sometimes forget what a great gift we have, and we take our Bibles for granted. It's easy for us to purchase Bibles or even get them for free, but it's not that way for all believers. Bibles are smuggled into some places or secretly printed. Some people groups do not have Bibles in their native tongue. And there are still some people who do not even have a written language.

What they wouldn't give to have just a portion of God's precious Word! Yet many of us take it for granted. We grab our Bible on Sunday morning and ignore it the rest of the week. Or we may give it a cursory glance on other days with little concern for what it says. We often leave our children's Bible training to their Sunday school teachers and pastors. Few of us actually pore over scripture seriously.

Oh, how God wants His children to study and live by the Bible! He wants so much for us to find strength from His Word. What pleasure He gains when He sees us mentoring others spiritually and sharing our own steps of faith with them.

We have great riches both in God's Word and in the gifts God has given us. Let's not take them lightly. The following passages deal with many aspects of God's Word. Read them carefully, and renew or establish your commitment to cherish the Bible.

⤳ *Perfection* ⤆

As for God, his way is perfect; the word
of the Lord is tried: he is a buckler
to all them that trust in him.
2 SAMUEL 22:31

Your way is perfect, oh Lord. You will never steer me wrong. When I face confusion in my life, I wonder what my next step should be, but Your Word guides me. It answers my questions about life, tells me how to handle relationships, instructs me in my role as a child of God, and encourages me daily. You have truly given me all I need to succeed.

❧ Sharing Faith with Children ❧

*And that from a child thou hast known
the holy scriptures, which are able to make
thee wise unto salvation through faith
which is in Christ Jesus.*
2 TIMOTHY 3:15

What a tremendous privilege I have to be able to share Your Word with children, dear God. It is an abundance of spiritual wealth right at our fingertips. Through scripture we can know Your great salvation and experience a deeper understanding of Your immense love for us. It is a prize to be treasured. Let us care for our Bibles, though the pages are worn from constant use!

❧ The Comfort of the Scriptures ❧

*For whatsoever things were written
aforetime were written for our learning,
that we through patience and comfort
of the scriptures might have hope.*
ROMANS 15:4

Lord, the world is not as You intended. You wanted us to glorify You—to have fellowship with You. Our twisted, sinful natures have caused sorrow and hate, fear and confusion. In Your great love

You've given me a way to have hope and comfort. You gave Your Word so I might learn how to have a restored relationship with You. I don't have to be defeated by the attitudes of this world. Through Your Word You've given me a better way.

⇥ Life through Christ's Name ⇤

But these are written, that ye might believe
that Jesus is the Christ, the Son of God;
and that believing ye might have
life through his name.

JOHN 20:31

We're such visual people, God. We should be able to accept who You are simply by faith, but You know how our minds work. We hold firm to the old saying "Seeing is believing." Even during biblical times people wanted a sign from You to prove who You were. So You gave us Your Word—a record of Your mighty acts—to help us know and believe in You. You looked ahead and saw what we would need, and You provided it.

✣ Words from God ✣

*I have manifested thy name unto the men which
thou gavest me out of the world: thine they were,
and thou gavest them me; and they have kept
thy word. Now they have known that all things
whatsoever thou hast given me are of thee.
For I have given unto them the words which
thou gavest me; and they have received them, and
have known surely that I came out from thee, and
they have believed that thou didst send me.*

JOHN 17:6–8

✣ No Void Returns ✣

*So shall my word be that goeth forth out of my mouth:
it shall not return unto me void, but it
shall accomplish that which I please, and
it shall prosper in the thing whereto I sent it.*

ISAIAH 55:11

Your Word is so effective, Father. Nothing is more
powerful. Oh God, if by Your Word You spoke the
world into existence, how can I doubt the power it
can have in my life? How can I question whether
it will influence the lives of others?

Let us feast on God's Word daily. It will do a
great work in us, for He has promised His Word
will not return unto Him void.

✦ Safety in God's Word ✦

Every word of God is pure: he is a shield unto
them that put their trust in him.
PROVERBS 30:5

Many dangers are lurking nearby, dear God. People
hate me for the stand I take for You. Satan hurls trials and temptations at me, but in Your Word I find
strength and safety. I know my friends are facing this
adversary, as well. Remind them they have protection
in You. We've often relied on our own strength for
these battles, but safety lies in Your Word.

✦ Hearing versus Doing ✦

But be ye doers of the word, and not hearers only,
deceiving your own selves.
JAMES 1:22

Father, I've seen children who look like they
are listening to their parents—they might even
acknowledge or repeat their words—but they fail
to put them into practice. Their behavior is frus-
trating at times, but I have to wonder how You
must feel. I am Your child. You've given me the
Bible to guide and protect me, yet I fail to live
by it. Forgive me, Lord. Make me a doer of Your
Word—not just a hearer.

✦ Growing Daily ✦

As newborn babes, desire the sincere milk of the word,
that ye may grow thereby.
1 PETER 2:2

In the spring when new lambs or cows are born, it is fun to watch them eagerly nurse from their mother. How instinctive and wonderful! Father, let me desire Your Word just as these young ones delight in that milk. Let it nourish and sustain me and bring continued growth.

✦ Meditation ✦

This book of the law shall not depart out of thy mouth;
but thou shalt meditate therein day and night,
that thou mayest observe to do according
to all that is written therein: for then
thou shalt make thy way prosperous, and
then thou shalt have good success.
JOSHUA 1:8

So many things demand my focus and attention, dear Jesus. There are times I'm not even sure how to handle situations. I love my role, and I know every season of life is a tremendous blessing. I want to do a good job fulfilling my responsibilities, and I'm grateful You've given me the Bible as my guidebook.

As I pore over each passage, it becomes more and more obvious that You want to help me succeed.

⤲ Keeping God's Word ⤪

*Blessed is he that readeth, and they that hear
the words of this prophecy, and keep those things
which are written therein: for the time is at hand.*
REVELATION 1:3

I know that my time on earth is limited and that what I do for You counts more than anything else. Ultimately it is You who will guide me in reading and living Your Word. All I can do is believe it and set the right example for those who watch. I want Your blessing in my life and in the lives of those I love. Help me to passionately study and obey Your commands.

⤲ God's Word Won't Change ⤪

*Ye shall not add unto the word which I command you,
neither shall ye diminish ought from it,
that ye may keep the commandments of
the LORD your God which I command you.*
DEUTERONOMY 4:2

Your Word is established forever, almighty God. A mere mortal, I've no business adding to or taking away from it. I would never deliberately take a pen and scratch through the parts that convict me. I wouldn't add words or lines here and there, but sometimes my life becomes that writing instrument as I choose to do my own thing. Forgive me, Father. I want my life to represent You according to Your whole Word—not just the parts I'm comfortable with.

✦ Hearing Leads to Trusting ✦

So then faith cometh by hearing,
and hearing by the word of God.
ROMANS 10:17

I want my friends and family to trust in You, Father, and I know You've given me the opportunity to be directly involved in their faith. I'm going to share Your Word with them daily. I will encourage them to memorize passages consistently. I commit to pray for their salvation and surrender them to You. Being able to take part in spreading the truths of the gospel is an amazing privilege. Lord, You've done so much for me; I want to give back to You.

→ Long-Lasting Word ←

Be ye mindful always of his covenant;
the word which he commanded
to a thousand generations.

1 CHRONICLES 16:15

I've had an old hymn running through my mind. It speaks of good, old-fashioned religion. One stanza says, "It was good for my mother and father, and it's good enough for me." I guess I don't know about "religion," so to speak, but Your Word was good for my parents and grandparents and generations before them. It's wonderful for me and the generations to follow. Your Word is all I need.

CHAPTER 3

My Joy: The Power of Fellowship with God

❧

And these things write we unto you,
that your joy may be full.
1 JOHN 1:4

We've all seen it—perhaps even worn it—the glow of having received good news. It's a perpetual smile and a lighter step. For the person who has just received good news, life is pure bliss. The little things—traffic, someone else's bad mood, rain—have no bearing on good news. Good news brightens the darkest day.

Nehemiah 12:43 says, "Also that day they offered great sacrifices, and rejoiced: for God had made them rejoice with great joy." Were the Israelites rejoicing because every day was happy? No. Were they living easy lives? Absolutely not! They'd been in captivity. Their beloved temple had been destroyed, and they'd faced terrible opposition as they tried to rebuild it. Worst of all, there was sin among them. From a worldly perspective, they had little to bring them joy. Yet when they repented of their sin, God caused them to rejoice.

Our joy comes from God. Never lose sight of this. Even when your days are pleasant, when your friends are kind and no one at home is ill, when all is right with your career, God is the source of true joy. As long as we walk faithfully with Him, we will find reasons to rejoice. His Word is full of descriptions of how to experience this wonderful blessing. Get to know these passages. You will be rewarded more richly than you have ever imagined.

→ I Will Rejoice ←

And ye now therefore have sorrow: but
I will see you again, and your heart shall rejoice,
and your joy no man taketh from you.
JOHN 16:22

You are with me, dear Jesus. What more could I wish? Just being with You today makes my heart sing, and it's a joy no one can steal from me. You have given it freely, and You want it to be mine. I cherish this treasure, and I want those around me to experience it, too. Let my life so exude Your joy that everyone I meet will desire You, too.

❧ Tidings of Great Joy ❧

And the angel said unto them, Fear not:
for, behold, I bring you good tidings of great joy,
which shall be to all people.

LUKE 2:10

Dear God, You remember how it was when I received good news. I couldn't wait to share it with everyone around me. My friends and my family graciously listened as I told them what I'd learned. Yet this glorious event in my life can't begin to compare with the joyful tidings proclaimed by the angels the night Your Son was born. It is Your Son who makes my life worth living!

❧ In Your Presence Is Joy ❧

I have set the LORD always before me: because he is
at my right hand, I shall not be moved. Therefore my
heart is glad, and my glory rejoiceth: my flesh also shall
rest in hope. For thou wilt not leave my soul in hell;
neither wilt thou suffer thine Holy One to see
corruption. Thou wilt shew me the path of life:
in thy presence is fulness of joy; at thy right hand
there are pleasures for evermore.

PSALM 16:8–11

✣ The Joy of the Lord Is My Strength ✣

For the joy of the LORD is your strength.
NEHEMIAH 8:10

I'm tired today, dear God. There have been moments when I thought I couldn't take another step. The truth is that I can't move forward without You. But You are with me. Your yoke is easy; Your burden is light. You want to take the pressure off me. What a joy it is for me to walk with You—to draw strength from You. What a wondrous gift to be in Your company.

✣ Fruit of the Spirit ✣

But the fruit of the Spirit is love, joy, peace, longsuffering, gentleness, goodness, faith, meekness, temperance: against such there is no law.
GALATIANS 5:22–23

I don't see how I could be Your child and not have joy in my life, dear God. Oh, I know I'm still subject to human emotions and problems, but You are at work in my soul. You will cultivate joy within me if I will let You. Then others will see it. My family, my friends—everyone will want You to be their gardener, too. Please let the soil of my heart be fertile for the seeds You want to sow.

⤞ An Obvious Command ⤝

Rejoice evermore.
1 THESSALONIANS 5:16

You really can't make it any clearer than this, can You, Lord? Forgive me, please. I'm often guilty of attaching addendums to this command. "Rejoice evermore. . .if the bills get paid." "Rejoice evermore. . .if no one gives me grief at work and if I get the promotion I deserve." I'm wrong, Lord. I've no business adding to Your perfect Word. You simply said, "Rejoice evermore." Period.

⤞ A Joyful Prayer ⤝

And Hannah prayed, and said, My heart rejoiceth
in the LORD, mine horn is exalted in the LORD:
my mouth is enlarged over mine enemies; because
I rejoice in thy salvation. There is none holy as the
LORD: for there is none beside thee: neither is there any
rock like our God. . . . They that were full have hired
out themselves for bread; and they that were hungry
ceased: so that the barren hath born seven; and
she that hath many children is waxed feeble.
1 SAMUEL 2:1–2, 5

✦ Painful Joy ✦

Behold, happy is the man whom God correcteth:
therefore despise not thou the chastening
of the Almighty.
JOB 5:17

Correction is never enjoyable, but I know You
sometimes need to discipline me to make me use-
ful for You. Oh, how it hurts at times, but what a
happy day it will be when You say to me, "Well
done, my faithful servant!" Help me understand
and appreciate the point of your correction.

✦ My Heart Rejoices ✦

My soul doth magnify the Lord, and my spirit hath
rejoiced in God my Saviour. For he hath regarded
the low estate of his handmaiden: for, behold, from
henceforth all generations shall call me blessed.
For he that is mighty hath done to me great things;
and holy is his name. And his mercy is on them that
fear him from generation to generation.
LUKE 1:46–50

✦ My Son Has Come Home ✦

For this my son was dead, and is alive
again; he was lost, and is found.
And they began to be merry.
LUKE 15:24

It's not easy to watch my child make mistakes, dear Father. I'm sure no one understands that better than You. I've messed up so many times, yet when I repent, You eagerly open Your arms and lovingly welcome me back. I guess that must be why I am able to joyfully embrace my son when he, too, seeks forgiveness. I have had the best example in You.

✦ God Gives Joy ✦

For God giveth to a man that is good
in his sight wisdom, and knowledge, and joy.
ECCLESIASTES 2:26

Oh, giver of all things good, how grateful I am that You have granted me godly happiness. I am truly undeserving of this blessing, but what refreshment it is to turn from the cares of everyday life and to be bathed in Your eternal joy! I am humbled when I recall how willingly You gave of Yourself that I might experience this pleasure.

✣ Restore Your Joy ✦

*Make me to hear joy and gladness; that the bones
which thou hast broken may rejoice.
Hide thy face from my sins, and blot out all
mine iniquities. Create in me a clean heart,
O God; and renew a right spirit within me.
Cast me not away from thy presence; and
take not thy holy spirit from me. Restore unto me
the joy of thy salvation; and uphold me with thy
free spirit. Then will I teach transgressors thy ways;
and sinners shall be converted unto thee.*

PSALM 51:8–13

✣ Sing with Gladness ✦

*Therefore the redeemed of the LORD shall return,
and come with singing unto Zion; and
everlasting joy shall be upon their head:
they shall obtain gladness and joy; and
sorrow and mourning shall flee away.*

ISAIAH 51:11

Blessed Redeemer, my heart is filled with rejoicing
as I consider Your finished work on Calvary and
at the garden tomb. Death and the grave have no
claim on me, for in You I have my victory. One day
I will leave the trials of this world behind and enter

the gates of heaven. Oh, what a day that will be! And what joy to know my loved ones will join me as we meet those who've gone before us. A great day is coming!

→ *Joy in God's Word* ←

*These things have I spoken unto you,
that my joy might remain in you,
and that your joy might be full.*
JOHN 15:11

You are my guide and instructor, dear God. I do not need to figure out how to live. Your precious Word tells me. It provides the insight I need to be a godly friend and family member in a manner that pleases You. You teach me how to serve You and to minister to others. You've given everything I need to live an abundant life, and You did it so my joy would be full. How glad I am to have a personal God.

CHAPTER 4

My Peace: The Power of Complete Trust in God

❧

Nicole was a young woman fully dedicated to Jesus. Her desire was to serve Him no matter what the cost, and that is how she and her husband became part of their college's traveling music ministry. On their way to a meeting, a much larger vehicle struck their van, and the whole group died instantly. It was a devastating time for many, but at Nicole's memorial service, her father made this statement: "We want you to know that we. . .are rejoicing because we know God makes no mistakes."

Wow! A statement like that can come only from a deep relationship with a heavenly Father who grants a peace that passes all understanding. *God makes no mistakes!* These young people were fully serving God, yet this same God allowed their lives to end abruptly. It seems ironic—even unfair—to us, but God sees the bigger picture. Accepting His sovereignty is what allows us to have peace even during times of great difficulty.

Yes, this wonderful woman probably would have continued to reach people for Christ, but we may never know how many lives she will have touched or how many souls will have accepted Christ as a result of the legacy she left and the blessed peace her family exhibited during what seemed a terrible tragedy.

God often works in unusual ways. We will not always comprehend what He is doing, and that is the beauty of the peace He offers. When our trust is fully in Him, and our friends and neighbors see what He does in our lives through both the good times and the bad, I can think of no greater testament to His love.

Are you resting in God's peace today, or are you fighting against or wallowing in the struggles of life? If you are trying to handle challenges alone, it is time to stop. Give them to God, who wants to bathe you in a peace only He can give.

⤳ *Perfect Peace* ⤶

Thou wilt keep him in perfect peace, whose mind is stayed on thee: because he trusteth in thee.
ISAIAH 26:3

This is a passage I think every Christian should memorize. Such a promise and a challenge are packed into this nugget of scripture. You want us to fill our souls with peace in spite of the terrors around us. If our focus is on You and Your omnipotence, we will trust You. You can envelop us in Your peace. What an amazing God You are!

☩ Peace in the Lord ☩

Hear me when I call, O God of my righteousness:
thou hast enlarged me when I was in distress;
have mercy upon me, and hear my prayer. . . .
There be many that say, Who will shew us any good?
LORD, lift thou up the light of thy countenance upon
us. Thou hast put gladness in my heart, more than in
the time that their corn and their wine increased.
I will both lay me down in peace, and sleep: for thou,
LORD, only makest me dwell in safety.
PSALM 4:1, 6–8

☩ The Quietness of God ☩

When he giveth quietness, who then can make trouble?
JOB 34:29

We witnessed an unbelievable storm last night. The first crash of thunder brought the children running. We talked about many aspects of the powerful storm. Soon they were excited rather than frightened, and their childish play escalated to new heights. Between their squeals and the storm, things were noisy. Suddenly the power ceased. Slowly the children crept to me, and I softly told the story of the time You calmed the storm. Their breathing slowed; they slept. Your peace filled our home in the midst of the storm.

✢ The Peace of God's Children ✤

And all thy children shall be taught of the LORD;
and great shall be the peace of thy children.
ISAIAH 54:13

I'm so glad You want to teach us, Lord. There is no teacher greater than You. When we learn from You, we will discover all we need to know about the world and the people around us. We will have no reason to fear, for we will have received our instruction from the Master. I dedicate myself to helping those I love discover the lessons You have for them so they can be at peace.

✢ To Be Spiritually Minded ✤

For to be carnally minded is death;
but to be spiritually minded is life and peace.
ROMANS 8:6

I've seen both sides of the mind's coin, Jesus. Before You saved me, I was drawn to sinful pleasures. They left me empty. After I accepted You and began to focus on godly things, I discovered new peace. This is what I want for my family. Although only You can save them, I can commit to protecting them from wickedness and surrounding them with purity as much as possible, and I ask You to make them spiritually minded.

☩ Strength and Peace ☩

The LORD will give strength unto his people;
the LORD will bless his people with peace.
PSALM 29:11

It's interesting the way You couple strength and peace. It almost seems as if they don't go together. Still, I am reminded of a father as he plays with his children. He's strong and could easily hurt them, but he loves them and keeps his strength under control. They feel safe and loved and at peace. That's how we feel in Your presence, Lord.

☩ Peaceable Wisdom ☩

But the wisdom that is from above is first pure, then
peaceable, gentle, and easy to be intreated, full of mercy
and good fruits, without partiality, and without hypocrisy.
JAMES 3:17

Many people claim their wisdom is from their god, but it seems that much of what they believe is evil. Thank You, Father, that Your wisdom is abundantly good. It brings joy and peace to my heart, but it extends even farther. When I apply Your wisdom to the decisions I make, it affects my family and others around me. It can contribute to their peace, too. Please give me this wisdom.

⋅ Live in Peace ⋅

Finally, brethren, farewell. Be perfect,
be of good comfort, be of one mind, live in peace;
and the God of love and peace shall be with you.
2 CORINTHIANS 13:11

We have a houseful of people with different personalities, ideas, and attitudes, dear God. Sometimes that can be a lot of fun, but it can also be confusing. Still, You've commanded us to live in peace, and of course, that's what we want, too. Please give us the ability to work together. Show us when we should compromise. Fill our home with love and peace.

⋅ Getting Along ⋅

If it be possible, as much as lieth in you,
live peaceably with all men.
ROMANS 12:18

I'm always trying to teach the children in my life to work out their differences with others in a peaceful, positive way. I know that to reinforce these lessons, I must do my best to love them. I realize it isn't always possible; some people thrive on being difficult. With Your help I will always try to work with those whose opinions differ from mine. I will try to find a suitable solution in each situation.

✦ Hope, Joy, and Peace ✦

*Now the God of hope fill you with all joy and
peace in believing, that ye may abound in hope,
through the power of the Holy Ghost.*
ROMANS 15:13

We just celebrated my son's birthday, dear God.
He was thrilled with the presents he received, and
we were happy to see his excitement. Still, there is
no way the best we could offer can compare to the
perfect hope, joy, and peace You give through the
Holy Spirit. These are lasting gifts that will bless
our lives forever. Let us receive them gladly.

✦ The Holy Ghost, My Comforter ✦

*These things have I spoken unto you, being yet
present with you. But the Comforter, which is the
Holy Ghost, whom the Father will send in my name,
he shall teach you all things, and bring all things to
your remembrance, whatsoever I have said unto you.
Peace I leave with you, my peace I give unto you: not
as the world giveth, give I unto you. Let not your heart
be troubled, neither let it be afraid. Ye have heard how
I said unto you, I go away, and come again unto you.
If ye loved me, ye would rejoice, because I said, I go
unto the Father: for my Father is greater than I.*
JOHN 14:25–28

❖ Paths of Peace ❖

Her ways are ways of pleasantness,
and all her paths are peace.
PROVERBS 3:17

All-knowing God, I realize Proverbs 3:17 is describing wisdom, but I would love for those words to describe me, too. A significant amount of peace is needed to live in this world and complete my daily tasks. I need to be able to handle my responsibilities with a calm spirit. I need to help my friends and family resolve their differences in a positive way. I need to handle the pressures of daily life with a serenity that comes from You. Lord, make my paths peaceable.

❖ Perfection and Peace ❖

Mark the perfect man, and behold the upright:
for the end of that man is peace.
PSALM 37:37

Everyone wants to experience peace, Lord. I'll admit I've tried more than one method of obtaining it. It's obvious that human attempts are limited at best. But You've made it clear that perfection leads to peace. "Impossible," many will say, but You aren't saying we'll never make mistakes. You're simply saying that if we walk according to Your Word and sincerely grow in faith, Your peace will result.

→ *Step Lively Now* ←

For ye shall go out with joy, and be led forth with peace: the mountains and the hills shall break forth before you into singing, and all the trees of the field shall clap their hands.
ISAIAH 55:12

I sit here staring out my kitchen window, Lord. Children and their dog are frolicking on the hill nearby. Their laughter fills the air. They are so carefree. I am reminded that when I walk with You, my step, too, will be lighter. You will take my cares upon You and embrace me with Your peace. The whole world is brighter when You are the center of my life.

CHAPTER 5

My Purpose: The Power of Positive Influence

✤

What is your purpose in life? Perhaps you are so busy fulfilling that purpose that you've never really given it much thought, but God has a perfect plan for each one of us. Some things He is very specific about. For instance, we are to praise God (Psalm 150:6). We are to worship God (Matthew 4:10). We are commanded to witness (Acts 1:8).

There are just some things that we as believers know we are to do. It's important to be faithful in these areas, because when we are, God is able to begin revealing what He has for us to do personally.

Did you realize that God set His purpose for you in place before you were even born (Jeremiah 1:5)? To some people that might seem a bit presumptuous. We like to be independent and free to make our own decisions. We need to remember that God created us. He knows us better than we know ourselves. Based on what He knows about us and the world around us, He designed a plan for each of us. We do have a choice to make. We must decide whether we will discover and fulfill God's purpose, thus attaining abundant joy, satisfaction, and eternal reward, or whether we will stumble about trying to do our own thing.

There are many different things we can do to glorify God, but if I'm upset because I think your duties are more glamorous than mine, I am not going to accomplish anything worthwhile. God did not plan for all of us to do the same thing (1 Corinthians 12), but each of us working together and doing our part for the Lord is what will draw people to Him.

Regardless of our roles in life, we should set an example of faithfulness for others to follow. If other people see us obeying God, they are more likely to do the same themselves. What if Zacharias and Elisabeth had refused to obey God? Would their son, John the Baptist, have been willing to live such a wild and rugged life and point so many to the Savior? Only God knows the answer, but the question is worth considering. Won't you ask God to show you what your purpose is and to help you fulfill it? Be faithful. As you are, He will reveal more and more of His plan for you.

✣ My Wages ✣

And in the same house remain, eating and drinking
such things as they give: for the labourer is worthy
of his hire. Go not from house to house.
LUKE 10:7

Parenthood has aptly been called a "labor of love."
The financial benefits may not exist, but the divi-
dends of the occupation cannot be matched. I have
the opportunity to teach my children that You love
them. I get to be a part of their acceptance of You.
You allow me to aid them in their spiritual growth
and understanding. As I watch them develop into
young people who honor You, I realize the com-
pensation of my life's work is beyond compare.

✣ Glorify God ✣

Whether therefore ye eat, or drink, or whatsoever
ye do, do all to the glory of God.
1 CORINTHIANS 10:31

I've read this passage too many times to count,
Lord, but I really needed it this morning. So many
little interruptions or daily detours in my schedule
tempt me to get frustrated or even angry. Sometimes the surprises prevent me from being where
I want to be, but You know best. You've given me

these interruptions and detours, and I need to honor You by doing my best. Please make my attitude right.

✦ Made to Praise the Lord ✦

*All thy works shall praise thee, O Lord; and
thy saints shall bless thee. They shall speak of
the glory of thy kingdom, and talk of thy power;
to make known to the sons of men his mighty acts,
and the glorious majesty of his kingdom.
Thy kingdom is an everlasting kingdom, and
thy dominion endureth throughout all generations.
The Lord upholdeth all that fall, and raiseth up all
those that be bowed down. The eyes of all wait upon
thee; and thou givest them their meat in due season.*
PSALM 145:10–15

✦ Created for a Purpose ✦

*For by him were all things created, that are in heaven,
and that are in earth, visible and invisible,
whether they be thrones, or dominions,
or principalities, or powers: all things
were created by him, and for him.*
COLOSSIANS 1:16

Dear Creator of all things, when You spoke this

world into existence, when You formed me with Your hands, they weren't just random acts of Your power. All creation, including me, is intended to glorify and praise You. I need to convey this message to those with whom I brush shoulders. They need to understand that they, too, are here to honor You. Together we can exalt Your name.

⇢ God's Instructions ⇠

And God blessed them, and God said unto them, Be fruitful, and multiply, and replenish the earth, and subdue it: and have dominion over the fish of the sea, and over the fowl of the air, and over every living thing that moveth upon the earth.
GENESIS 1:28

From the earliest days of creation, You have been specific about what You want us to do, Lord. You said You want me to care for the earth in a way that pleases You. I want to learn what I can about Your creation so that I can appreciate it in all its splendor.

✦ Loving God ✦

*He that loveth father or mother more than me
is not worthy of me: and he that loveth son or
daughter more than me is not worthy of me.*
MATTHEW 10:37

Oh God, one of my favorite times of day is when
my young daughter awakens. I go into her room,
and she stands there reaching for me with the most
beautiful smile. I feel her love immediately. While
I'm glad my child delights in me, it is infinitely
more important that she learns to love You. Help
me to point her in that direction.

✦ The Results of the Rod of Reproof ✦

*The rod and reproof give wisdom: but a child left
to himself bringeth his mother to shame.*
PROVERBS 29:15

Children have big ideas, Lord. They want to do
things their own way. I know that leaving them to
their own designs could be quite disastrous. I, too,
can start to think my ideas and plans are better
than Yours. Please give me the direction and discipline I need to properly obey what You've carefully
included in Your Word.

⋆ A Shining Light ⋆

That ye may be blameless and harmless,
the sons of God, without rebuke, in the midst
of a crooked and perverse nation, among
whom ye shine as lights in the world.
PHILIPPIANS 2:15

Light makes me feel good, Father. I love it when the sun comes streaming through my windows. When the day ends, I'm glad to be able to turn on the lights and promote a cheerful atmosphere in my home. Light offers hope. That's what I want to do. I want to draw people to You. I want my friends and neighbors and even people I don't know to see You in me. Let me be a light for You, Father.

⋆ My Testimony ⋆

Having your conversation honest among the Gentiles:
that, whereas they speak against you as evildoers, they
may by your good works, which they shall behold,
glorify God in the day of visitation.
1 PETER 2:12

Father, by Your grace You saved me. My life is not what it was at the beginning. Salvation is a grand gift, but You don't want me to keep it to myself.

You always planned for me to share it. Many people won't want it. They'll look for evidence in my life to discredit all I say. Help me to live in such a way that they won't find anything. My purpose is to draw them to You. Let my life and speech do just that.

❖ When Others Are in Charge ❖

Let as many servants as are under the yoke count their own masters worthy of all honour, that the name of God and his doctrine be not blasphemed.
1 TIMOTHY 6:1

Last night when I told my son to clean his room, his lower lip shot out. "This is *not* fun," he complained. "Maybe not, but it's a job that needs done," I replied. I thought about the way my boss sometimes asks me to do jobs that aren't fun. I could complain and blow my testimony, but I know I should just do the work cheerfully, realizing that it's helpful to someone else. In this way I will bring glory to You.

⇨ Be Holy ⇦

Speak unto all the congregation of the children
of Israel, and say unto them, Ye shall be holy:
for I the LORD your God am holy.
LEVITICUS 19:2

Dear God, I don't know how many times I have
said to my children, "Do this." They say, "Why?" I
flippantly respond, "Because I said so." In reality
I should be setting the example. You've told me
to be perfect because You're perfect. My children
need to understand that I don't have double standards. I will determine to be a positive influence.

⇨ His Mother Taught Him ⇦

The words of king Lemuel, the prophecy
that his mother taught him.
PROVERBS 31:1

I can appreciate these writings of Lemuel, dear
God. Here's a grown man—a king—and he readily admits that something his mother taught
him had value. Parents often seek to guide their
grown children the wrong way. Help us to handle
situations properly so they know we love them.
Although they won't always follow our sugges-
tions, help our children to trust and follow You.

⟿ *Sleep as a Reward* ⟾

The sleep of a labouring man is sweet, whether he eat little or much: but the abundance of the rich will not suffer him to sleep.

ECCLESIASTES 5:12

It was a busy day, Lord, and truthfully I'm exhausted, but I feel great. This morning my toddler joined me in window washing. It took extra time with her in tow, but what a blast! When my older children arrived home from school, we worked in the garden and enjoyed some of the results for supper. What a day! You intend for me to work hard. Now I know I'll get a good night's sleep.

CHAPTER 6

My Finances: The Power of Good Stewardship

∞

Rhonda planned, organized, and held a garage sale. She made a decent amount of money that she intended to use as her Christmas fund. Soon after, she learned her church was having a special offering for a family in need. Rhonda and her husband prayed about how much to give. In a last-minute decision, she placed all of the garage sale money in the offering.

A short time later, Rhonda was involved in an automobile accident. She wasn't injured, but her vehicle needed repair. She received some estimates, and the insurance check was issued. In the end the repairs cost far less than originally thought, and she was able to keep the extra money—an amount far in excess of the amount given in that special offering.

God does work in amazing ways. Often we don't understand what He is doing, but His ways are perfect. Each of us has a different financial situation. By the world's standards some of us are quite well-to-do. Others struggle to make ends meet; many of us are somewhere in the middle.

God has quite a bit to say about our finances. First of all, whether we are rich or poor, our money belongs to Him. He expects us to be good stewards of what He has given us (Matthew 25:14–30). He also expects us to have the right attitude about money. Matthew 6:19–21 reminds us that laying up treasure in heaven is infinitely more worthwhile than storing up goods on earth.

Do you remember the story of the rich but foolish landowner in Luke 12:16–21? God blessed him abundantly. However, instead of thanking God, the foolish man took all the credit and decided to spend the next several years irresponsibly. He forgot that God was still in control, and God's plans were different. What a shame he squandered God's blessing.

We parents sometimes get preoccupied with our financial situations. We shouldn't, though. God has given us plenty of advice in His Word. We just need to spend time talking to Him about it.

⇥ Great Riches ⇤

There is that maketh himself rich, yet hath nothing:
there is that maketh himself poor, yet hath great riches.
PROVERBS 13:7

Lord, sometimes I'm tempted to envy those with "things." I begin thinking about how much easier life would be if I just made more money. Then I consider what that would involve. We'd share fewer family meals. I'd rarely do the things I really love because I would be busy at work. As I look at it that way, I realize what wonderful riches I have.

⇥ A Willing Heart ⇤

Speak unto the children of Israel, that they bring me
an offering: of every man that giveth it willingly
with his heart ye shall take my offering.
EXODUS 25:2

Make my heart willing, Lord, for it's the only way my gift will be blessed. Our church has asked for financial contributions that really are needed. I intend to give toward the need, but I want to do it out of true desire and not because I feel guilty. Part of me wants to hold back so I can use the money for something else, but I know that when I give to Your work, everyone benefits. God, please make my giving pure.

☩ A Changed Heart ☩

And Zacchaeus stood, and said unto the Lord:
Behold, Lord, the half of my goods I give to the poor;
and if I have taken any thing from any man by
false accusation, I restore him fourfold. And Jesus said
unto him, This day is salvation come to this house,
forsomuch as he also is a son of Abraham. For the Son
of man is come to seek and to save that which was lost.

LUKE 19:8–10

☩ Blessed Be the Name of the Lord ☩

Naked came I out of my mother's womb, and
naked shall I return thither: the LORD gave,
and the LORD hath taken away;
blessed be the name of the LORD.

JOB 1:21

Father, when Job spoke these words, he'd already faced horrible tragedy, but the worst was yet to come. I am always amazed that even as he begged for an explanation, he never turned his back on You. He realized nothing was really his, so although his losses were painful, he was able to endure.

I know that difficulties are inevitable. You give and take away as You see fit, and I must bless You.

❖ Robbery! ❖

Will a man rob God? Yet ye have robbed me.
But ye say, Wherein have we robbed thee?
In tithes and offerings.
MALACHI 3:8

Sirens screamed throughout my house. A silver badge flashed briefly as little hands grabbed my wrists. "You're under arrest! You robbed the bank!" And I was led away to the bedroom jailhouse. As I pondered the comical scene, I realized I would never rob a bank or steal from a store. Yet how many times have I robbed You, Lord? When I fail to give tithes and offerings, I rob You. Please forgive me.

❖ Caesar ❖

Then saith he unto them, Render therefore
unto Caesar the things which are Caesar's;
and unto God the things that are God's.
MATTHEW 22:21

Every time I vote there seems to be some levy on the ballot. Sometimes they are good levies; other times they are questionable. Still, I'm glad I can vote, and when taxes do get passed, I need to take responsibility and pay them. I must set the example and be a good testimony to others. Lord, please help me not to complain, and please provide for our needs.

⤳ *The Question of Loans* ⤆

My son, if thou be surety for thy friend,
if thou hast stricken thy hand with a stranger,
thou art snared with the words of thy mouth,
thou art taken with the words of thy mouth.
PROVERBS 6:1–2

Lord, how I want my friends and family to become financially responsible individuals. I'd like to be able to cosign on loans for their first cars or real estate; I'd even like to be able to provide the loan when possible, but I need to know I won't regret it. I need to be sure that this won't harm the relationship. Please provide the wisdom I need.

⤳ *Stir My Heart* ⤆

And they came, every one whose heart stirred him up,
and every one whom his spirit made willing,
and they brought the LORD's offering to the
work of the tabernacle of the congregation,
and for all his service, and for the holy garments.
EXODUS 35:21

It's exciting to have some small part in increasing

Your kingdom, God. At times it seems hard to let go of that hard-earned extra bit of cash, but what joy when I do! Although I don't always know exactly how that offering will be used when I drop it in the plate at church, I do know that its ultimate purpose will be to bring souls to You. So stir my heart, Father. Make me a willing giver.

✦ The Joy of Giving ✦

Upon the first day of the week let every one of you lay by him in store, as God hath prospered him, that there be no gatherings when I come.
1 CORINTHIANS 16:2

Dear God, it's the holiday season. It looks as though my family will have a nice Christmas, but for some in our church, there might not be gifts under the tree. I'd like to use this opportunity to appreciate the joy of giving. Help all of us to remember that as You bless us, we should bless others. And thank You for the greatest gift ever known—Jesus.

✦ More Than Enough ✦

And they spake unto Moses, saying, The people bring
much more than enough for the service of the work,
which the Lord commanded to make.

EXODUS 36:5

Oh Lord, has there been a time in recent history
that Your people have brought more than enough
for Your work? Everything costs so much these
days, Father. Updates, repairs, insurance, small
supplies—nothing is free, but much is worthwhile. If You'll do a work in our hearts, we Your
people will bring more than enough. We'll abundantly offer our time, talents, and finances, and
we'll leave a godly heritage for the generations
to follow.

✦ Treasure in Heaven ✦

Jesus said unto him, If thou wilt be perfect,
go and sell that thou hast, and give to the poor,
and thou shalt have treasure in heaven:
and come and follow me.

MATTHEW 19:21

Good Master, how sad You must have been the day
the wealthy young man turned his back on You in
favor of his riches. How often do I hurt You by

putting "things" before my relationship with You?
I don't have great wealth, but at times my attitude
isn't much different than this man's. Forgive me,
Jesus. I want to follow You fully.

✦ Sowing and Reaping ✦

But this I say, He which soweth sparingly shall reap
also sparingly; and he which soweth bountifully
shall reap also bountifully.
2 CORINTHIANS 9:6

You know how much I enjoy my garden, Lord.
From the smell of freshly tilled soil to the first
seedlings and the earliest harvest, each moment is
a reward in its own right. How exciting, too, to see
missionaries on the field, kids saved through children's ministries, and outreach programs begun,
and to know I had a part through my prayers and
finances. As we abundantly sow our garden, let us
also abundantly sow seeds for Your harvest.

☩ Be Content ☩

Let your conversation be without covetousness;
and be content with such things as ye have:
for he hath said, I will never leave thee,
nor forsake thee.
HEBREWS 13:5

I don't understand, Lord. So often I'm tempted to complain. Little things discourage me. I see the gifts that others have received from You and wonder why You haven't given them to me. But then I remember that You are a gift and You've given me far more than I deserve. Help me to be content.

☩ God Meets My Needs ☩

But my God shall supply all your need according
to his riches in glory by Christ Jesus.
PHILIPPIANS 4:19

Sometimes I have a hard time differentiating between needs and wants. I might say, "I need a new dishwasher," when a bottle of detergent and a dish rag would work. I might say, "I need a bigger house," when in reality I have too much stuff. Father, I know You truly will provide for my needs. Thank You.

CHAPTER 7

My Service: The Power of a Willing Heart

∞

There is no doubt that God expects us to willingly serve Him and others. It seems, though, that there is a fine line between what is good and what is too much. Certainly God wants us to attend church and share the gospel with others. There is some area in our churches for each of us to work. Service also can extend to participating in a community project or meeting a neighbor's need. It includes being a friend and offering a listening ear. Many types of ministry and service bring glory to God. They might involve time, money, or sacrifice, but being a blessing to others is worth it.

There is such a thing as doing too much, though. Serving others while ignoring the needs of your family, for instance, can have damaging effects. I have known people who were so busy with their commitments that they virtually lost their kids. This is not what God intended. God has given us stewardship of all that He has entrusted to us, and He expects us to apply His wisdom in our relationship with them. If we don't obey God, how can we expect Him to bless our efforts?

The area of service requires much prayer. We need to ask God where He wants us to volunteer, and we need to ask for strength and stamina to do all things well. Christ, our best example, came to be a servant, but even He took time to rest and to spend time with those closest to Him. He also involved His disciples in His work. So when we're considering what we might do, why not think about ways we can involve our families? If you volunteer to clean your church, take some kids along to help, and stop for ice cream afterward. If there's a need for Sunday school teachers, find a class you and your spouse can co-teach. God loves a willing heart. How much more must a willing family please Him?

⋗ Muddy Feet ⋖

If I then, your Lord and Master, have washed your feet; ye also ought to wash one another's feet.
JOHN 13:14

Recently we have had a good deal of rain, and the children have been thoroughly enjoying the mud. It's been a blast to watch them, but it's made for some very filthy kids. As I scrubbed the mud from between little toes, I thought about Your example when You washed the disciples' feet. I want to follow Your lead. I want to bless my family and others. I only ask for a servant's heart.

✦ Gladness ✦

I was glad when they said unto me,
Let us go into the house of the LORD.
PSALM 122:1

I'm ashamed to admit I don't always feel glad about going to church, Lord. I know I need to go to be encouraged and to be an encouragement, but sometimes I feel as though it's just one more thing on my to-do list. Please give me a better attitude. Restore the gladness that comes from fellowship with other believers. There is so much I can give and gain.

✦ Teaching Children to Serve ✦

And the child did minister unto the LORD
before Eli the priest.
1 SAMUEL 2:11

I am extremely busy. There are some tasks I could be teaching younger generations to perform, but so often it's easier to do them myself. God, I know You are continually working on me to make me a better servant. I cannot refuse to do the same for others. They might balk at it as I often do, but together we'll be works in progress.

⤋ Bring Forth Fruit ⤋

Herein is my Father glorified, that ye bear much fruit;
so shall ye be my disciples.
JOHN 15:8

We watched and waited, and we were so excited
when beans and radishes poked through the earth.
We saw onions, peas, and lettuce, and we cheered.
But where was the sweet corn? We replanted and
waited. Soon we were rewarded. I'm glad we didn't
give up. Let us be as diligent as we sow and nurture
gospel seeds. We want to glorify You in the abundance of fruit we bring to You.

⤋ A Lesson from Dorcas ⤋

Now there was at Joppa a certain disciple named
Tabitha, which by interpretation is called Dorcas:
this woman was full of good works
and almsdeeds which she did.
ACTS 9:36

Before Dorcas died, she was apparently known
only to her community, but she was loved for her
giving heart. She honored You, and You wanted to
use her further, so You raised her from the dead.
She must have been more popular then. Perhaps
people heard what had happened and were saved.

I'd like to be able to claim Philippians 1:24–25 with Dorcas and Paul. To die is to be with Christ, but to remain on earth is to be a blessing to others.

→ Building the Church ←

And have ye not read this scripture;
The stone which the builders rejected is
become the head of the corner.
MARK 12:10

I am privileged to be part of a special building project, and You are the chief cornerstone, dear Jesus. You dwell among this body of believers—Your church—and bless it in innumerable ways. We are a work in progress. We are Your bride, and we will not be complete until You come to take us to heaven. Keep us pure, and let us be a body of believers who will draw others to You.

☙ Labor of Love ❧

*For God is not unrighteous to forget your work
and labour of love, which ye have shewed
toward his name, in that ye have ministered
to the saints, and do minister.*

HEBREWS 6:10

Sometimes it seems as if being a parent is all labor; other times it's all love. Usually it's a balance of the two. In any case, it is very time-consuming. I don't always have the time or the energy to serve others as I would like to, and I feel guilty. Yet I am reminded that ministering to my children is a high calling. You will not overlook it, and You will bless me when I can help others.

☙ The Proper Attitude ❧

*But lay up for yourselves treasures in heaven, where
neither moth nor rust doth corrupt, and where
thieves do not break through nor steal.*

MATTHEW 6:20

I need wisdom in teaching others the proper attitude about service, God. I want them to have a healthy amount of pride in their work so they will do their best. At the same time, they need to understand that human praise pales in comparison to the joy that comes from pleasing You. It's a touchy situation. Please give me guidance.

☀ *The Courage of a Child* ☀

But Peter and John answered and said unto them,
Whether it be right in the sight of God to hearken
unto you more than unto God, judge ye.
For we cannot but speak the things
which we have seen and heard.
ACTS 4:19–20

In Sunday school my daughter made a gospel caterpillar. It consisted of different-colored circles, each representing some aspect of the Christian faith. When she asked for materials to reproduce it at home, I gave them to her, figuring it would entertain her for a while. I had no idea she'd make one for each of her school classmates. "They need to know Jesus, too," she said. Oh, to have such determination to witness.

✦ Tried by Fire ✦

Every man's work shall be made manifest:
for the day shall declare it, because it shall be
revealed by fire; and the fire shall try every
man's work of what sort it is.
1 CORINTHIANS 3:13

The promise of a trip to the pool put my children in motion. The deal was that their rooms first had to be cleaned to my satisfaction. Fifteen minutes later they returned. My son's room passed easily. While my daughter's floor was clean, the contents were piled onto her bed, and her comforter was draped over them. Her room did not pass. I know You'll try my works, too, Lord. Oh, how I want to please You.

✦ Important Jobs ✦

We have many members in one body,
and all members have not the same office.
ROMANS 12:4

Lord, it's amazing how often the lessons I share with people around me end up speaking volumes to my heart. For instance, recently I told someone that not taking his share of a responsibility at work would put too much pressure on someone else to get it done. Suddenly I thought about the fact that when I ignore my responsibilities at church, someone else has to step in. All jobs are important, and I should take mine seriously, too.

✦ With Christ Living in Us ✦

I am crucified with Christ: nevertheless I live;
yet not I, but Christ liveth in me: and
the life which I now live in the flesh I live by
the faith of the Son of God, who loved me,
and gave himself for me.
GALATIANS 2:20

We've been praying hard for one of our friends to receive You, Lord. We share the gospel with her, and week after week we invite her to church. She's just so afraid of what she'll have to give up if she accepts You. Oh Lord, help her to see what she will gain if she does allow You to live within her. Open her eyes so that she'll understand that living with You truly is life.

❖ Required to Be Faithful ❖

Moreover it is required in stewards,
that a man be found faithful.
1 CORINTHIANS 4:2

Master, You've given me stewardship over so many precious gifts—my family, my home, my ministries. You expect me to care for these blessings and serve them faithfully. You put them in my care for a specific reason. They belong to You, and I must treat them that way. Lord, give me the wisdom to carry out the duties You have given me. I so desire to hear You say one day, "Well done, good and faithful servant."

❖ Too Late ❖

The harvest is past, the summer is ended,
and we are not saved.
JEREMIAH 8:20

Yesterday I picked many quarts of strawberries. I thrilled at the sight of my baskets filling with ripe red fruit, but even as I picked, I discovered rotten, mushy berries on the plants or lying on the ground. It was too late to enjoy them. Oh God, how many lives have gone to waste because I waited too long to witness? You've given me a priceless lesson from the overripe berries. Let me never forget it.

Chapter 8

My Faith: The Power of Hope in God

❧

"Thank You that we're going to go swimming," my five-year-old confidently prayed. It was a praise full of faith. The reason: at that point we had no plans whatsoever of going swimming. He was hopeful, though, and he was trusting God to fulfill his desires.

It's easy for us to smile at the innocence of such prayers, but I have a feeling God smiles for a far different reason. The faith of a young child pleases Him. That's why He said if we want to accept Christ, we must become as a little child (Mark 10:15). A young child's faith is so sincere. He hasn't become so full of pride that he believes he can do everything on his own. He places his hope in God and realizes that it's God who meets his needs.

Since becoming a parent, I have learned a lot, and my children have been the ones who have taught me. William Wordsworth said, "The child is the father of the man." In other words, we can learn a lot about life and faith from the precious babes with whom we've been blessed.

You see, had it been me, I probably would have

said, "Lord, I'd really like to go swimming today. If it's Your will, please give us that opportunity." There's nothing wrong with that prayer, but it speaks only of possibility. It doesn't show a hope based on a complete trust that God is going to answer my prayer.

We also might be tempted to argue that God really isn't interested in simple things such as whether we go swimming. Why teach or encourage our children to pray about such things? Matthew 10:30 tells us God knows exactly how many hairs are on each one of our heads. If He takes note of such a tiny detail, we have every reason to believe He cares about every area of our lives, from the biggest to the smallest.

Sometimes we're just too proud or embarrassed to accept that truth. We trust Him with our eternal souls and with our big problems or decisions, but we fear He will laugh at us or scold us if we waste time on minor details. That's not how God works, though. We start out with a small seed of faith. We begin talking to God about each area of life. The more time we spend with Him, the more our faith grows. We just need to decide to hope in God.

Oh, that we could learn from our children!

✦ A Reason to Believe ✦

*Looking unto Jesus the author and finisher of our
faith; who for the joy that was set before him endured
the cross, despising the shame, and is set down
at the right hand of the throne of God.*
HEBREWS 12:2

You are the best example of faith I could hope for,
Lord Jesus. You knew all that You would face, and
You went through with it anyway. All that You've
ever done or will do gives me a reason to trust You.
I can recall many times that I've been blessed when
I've trusted in You, and I know that one day I'll
receive the ultimate reward—eternity with You.

✦ And Thy House ✦

*And they said, Believe on the Lord Jesus Christ,
and thou shalt be saved, and thy house.*
ACTS 16:31

Lord, I understand children aren't automatically
saved simply because their parents accepted You, but
when parents exhibit an unadulterated confidence in
You, children are sure to notice it and more likely to
trust You than if the parents had only a casual faith.
I've experienced much joy in my walk with You;
help me to demonstrate it in my walk with You.

✢ According to His Will ✦

And this is the confidence that we have in him,
that, if we ask any thing according
to his will, he heareth us.

1 JOHN 5:14

"Can I have candy? Can I have a car? Can I buy these shoes?" Children ask for things all day that wouldn't necessarily be of benefit to them at the time. Lord, I know I've asked You for things in the past even when I knew they weren't good for me; but when I pray according to Your will, You hear and answer abundantly. Thank You!

✢ Live by Faith ✦

For therein is the righteousness of God revealed
from faith to faith: as it is written,
The just shall live by faith.

ROMANS 1:17

I just received a letter from our missionary friends and shared bits of it with my family. My friends talked about the new building being erected for their church. As I read, my son asked, "Where do they get the money?" I explained that different churches helped them. "What if the churches don't?" he asked. Father, it was the perfect opportunity to explain that the just live by faith and that You provide for their needs.

✦ By Grace through Faith ✦

For by grace are ye saved through faith;
and that not of yourselves: it is the gift of God:
not of works, lest any man should boast.
EPHESIANS 2:8–9

Lord, You saved me because You love me. My salvation is by grace through faith, and no amount of good or bad behavior changes that. Thank You.

✦ God Will Fight Our Battles ✦

With him is an arm of flesh; but with us
is the LORD our God to help us,
and to fight our battles.
2 CHRONICLES 32:8

Dear God, I want to live according to the instructions You have given, but at times it seems I'm in the front lines of a very heated battle. This world's standards are not based on Your Word, and they make it increasingly difficult to do right. You are on my side. My confidence is in You, and You will be victorious.

✦ *Wait for the Promise* ✦

Behold, his soul which is lifted up is not upright
in him: but the just shall live by his faith.
HABAKKUK 2:4

"When are we going to heaven?" a four-year-old
asked. You know how hard it is for small children
to grasp these things. I assured her You know the
right time. "Well, I'm ready to go now so I won't
have to eat my vegetables." It was humorous, God,
but it was also an opportunity to teach her that
You always keep Your promises. We don't always
know how or when, but we trust that You will keep
them.

✦ *Victory* ✦

For whatsoever is born of God overcometh the world:
and this is the victory that overcometh
the world, even our faith.
1 JOHN 5:4

✦ *The Great Debate* ✦

That your faith should not stand in the wisdom
of men, but in the power of God.

1 CORINTHIANS 2:5

My children are young, Father, and right now they believe most of what I tell them. They accept that You created us and the rest of the world. They have confidence in Your power. The day will come all too soon when their beliefs will be challenged by "the wisdom of men." Establish their faith in You now, Lord. Help them to understand that true wisdom comes from You.

✦ *Safety* ✦

As for God, his way is perfect; the word
of the LORD is tried: he is a buckler
to all them that trust in him.

2 SAMUEL 22:31

As the mother of boys, I don't find it unusual to step on little green plastic army guys. Generally I'm too heavy, and they suffer a fatal blow. If they'd been in their jar where they belonged, they would have survived. It reminds me of the safety I have in You. The weight of the world can deliver crushing blows, but when my trust is in You where it belongs, I am safe.

✦ Great Tasting ✦

O taste and see that the LORD is good:
blessed is the man that trusteth in him.
PSALM 34:8

As a child, some of my favorite Bible lessons centered on Psalm 34:8. I enjoyed assembling the lollipop-and-pipe-cleaner crafts and learning how the treats are made. Mostly I think I enjoyed sampling different kinds of candy. The greatest lesson I learned is that a relationship with You is much sweeter than sugar, and the blessings of faith in You are much better than sweets.

✦ With All Your Heart ✦

Trust in the LORD with all thine heart; and
lean not unto thine own understanding.
PROVERBS 3:5

Lord, from the time my children were babies, I've committed them to Your care. When they were quite small, they looked to me for all the answers. As they grow, they realize that I don't know everything. I want them to understand, however, that You do and that everything is in Your control. Help them to commit daily to trusting You and to recognize that they don't have to face life alone.

✦ Being Fruitful ✦

*Blessed is the man that trusteth in the LORD,
and whose hope the LORD is. For he shall be
as a tree planted by the waters, and that
spreadeth out her roots by the river, and
shall not see when heat cometh, but her leaf
shall be green; and shall not be careful in the year
of drought, neither shall cease from yielding fruit.*

JEREMIAH 17:7–8

It's been a dry spring so far, Lord, and the garden is suffering as a result. I have enjoyed filling my bucket with water and distributing it among the plants. As the struggling plants soak up the life-giving refreshment, I think about the way that the lives of those who trust in You absorb the living water and are fruitful beyond imagination.

✦ Believe Only ✦

*But when Jesus heard it, he answered him,
saying, Fear not: believe only,
and she shall be made whole.*

LUKE 8:50

"Only believe." It sounds simple, Jesus, but this child was dead! I can't imagine how this man must have felt, but he obeyed. He allowed You to return to his home, so he must have had a certain amount of faith already. How greatly that faith must have increased as he witnessed the miraculous resurrection of his daughter.

CHAPTER 9

My Love: The Power of a Selfless Heart

∞

There are many kinds of love. We say we love hot fudge sundaes, but that isn't what we mean. We might really enjoy hot fudge sundaes, but saying we love them is using the word too lightly. We say we love dogs, and that is possible. We care for them. We spend time with them, but our affection for them doesn't exceed our love for our families.

We love other people but probably not in the same way we love our own family. We might go out of our way to show others we care, but most of us would do more for our own children than we would for someone else's.

No matter what kind of love we have, it is limited. We are finite; compared to God, we are capable of offering only a small amount of love. Maybe that's why it is sometimes hard to comprehend the love of God. Romans 5:7–8 offers a glimpse into the depth of God's love: "For scarcely for a righteous man will one die: yet peradventure for a good man some would even dare to die. But God commendeth his love toward us, in that, while we were yet sinners, Christ died for us."

Charles Wesley captured the greatness of God's love in the hymn "And Can It Be?" He asks, "And can it be that I should gain an interest in my Savior's love?" We have an interest in—a portion of—God's love. All the love in our hearts doesn't come close to even that portion of love God has for me.

That should be a challenge to us. Our love can grow on a regular basis if we love through Christ. Take some time to read and meditate on the book of 1 John. Doing so will strengthen the love in your heart.

⇥ *With All My Life* ⇤

And thou shalt love the LORD thy God with all thine heart, and with all thy soul, and with all thy might.
DEUTERONOMY 6:5

Jehovah God, You are the creator of all. Your power cannot be exceeded. You are above all, yet You want a personal love relationship with me. This truth is hard to comprehend, yet You require my total, undivided love. You want my entire devotion—my heart, soul, and strength. I cannot deny them. You, who have given me both physical and spiritual life, deserve only my best.

✣ Follow Charity ✣

Flee also youthful lusts: but follow righteousness,
faith, charity, peace, with them that call
on the Lord out of a pure heart.
2 TIMOTHY 2:22

During my teen years I faced a lot of pressure to fit in.
It wasn't always easy to follow examples of righteousness, faith, love, and peace. I learned an invaluable
lesson. It's important to establish strong standards
and convictions now, so that when temptation comes,
I will choose love for You over lust of the flesh.

✣ Misdirected Love ✣

Love not the world, neither the things that are
in the world. If any man love the world,
the love of the Father is not in him.
1 JOHN 2:15

Are my affections improper, dear Jesus? Am I too
committed to the things of this world—my job,
my friends, my hobbies? Oh, I know these things
have their proper place, but they should come after
my love for You. Is it possible that I'm entertaining
affection for things that should not be part of my
life at all? Please make them clear to me and help
me to eliminate them, for I want Your love in me.

⬦ A Love that Hurts ⬦

*And she went, and sat her down over against him a
good way off, as it were a bow shot: for she said,
Let me not see the death of the child.
And she sat over against him,
and lift up her voice, and wept.*

GENESIS 21:16

Oh God, how it must have hurt Hagar to know
the son she cherished was suffering. He'd been cast
from his father, and now he would die of thirst. It
was more than she could bear. Let us all remember
that healing—both physical and spiritual—comes
from You.

⬦ My First Love ⬦

*Nevertheless I have somewhat against thee,
because thou hast left thy first love.*

REVELATION 2:4

Forgive me, Lord Jesus. You have not been first place
in my life as You should be. I've given too many
excuses for why this might be so, but what it really
comes down to is that my love has weakened. I've
allowed too many things to come between us. I've
been wrong, and I'm sorry. Let me be on fire for You
once more. I want to return to You, my first love.

✢ The Greatest Gift ✢

For God so loved the world, that he gave
his only begotten Son, that whosoever
believeth in him should not perish,
but have everlasting life.
JOHN 3:16

I think perhaps John 3:16 is the most famous passage in Your Word. For what good would the rest of Your Word be if it weren't for Your precious gift and amazing sacrifice? Although I cannot fully grasp Your love, I thank You for it.

✢ Love and Correction ✢

For whom the LORD loveth he correcteth;
even as a father the son in whom he delighteth.
PROVERBS 3:12

❖ Getting the Right Order ❖

*He that loveth father or mother more than me is not
worthy of me: and he that loveth son or daughter
more than me is not worthy of me.*

MATTHEW 10:37

Oh Lord, I love my husband and adore my
children. It's hard to imagine anyone or anything
to whom I'd rather devote my time, but I need to
make sure my priorities are straight. Help me to
ensure that the time I give them doesn't take away
from what I give You. Oh, give me a desire to make
You first.

❖ Serving God in Love ❖

*But take diligent heed to do the commandment
and the law, which Moses the servant of the LORD
charged you, to love the LORD your God,
and to walk in all his ways, and to keep his
commandments, and to cleave unto him,
and to serve him with all your heart
and with all your soul.*

JOSHUA 22:5

Lord, I understand true love involves service; that
is the object of love. At times, though, my respon-

sibilities make overwhelming demands, and I become frustrated that I can't even sit down to a meal without thinking of something I need to do. I have to recognize that love involves service and sacrifice. It's true of my love for You, too. I must serve You 100 percent always.

☙ Charity ❧

Though I speak with the tongues of men and of angels, and have not charity, I am become as sounding brass, or a tinkling cymbal. . . . Charity suffereth long, and is kind; charity envieth not; charity vaunteth not itself, is not puffed up. . .beareth all things, believeth all things, hopeth all things, endureth all things. . . . And now abideth faith, hope, charity, these three; but the greatest of these is charity.
1 CORINTHIANS 13:1, 4, 7, 13

☙ Abounding Love ❧

And this I pray, that your love may abound yet more and more in knowledge and in all judgment.
PHILIPPIANS 1:9

I don't think anything is more powerful than love. When I enter my baby's room in the morning and

I see her angelic smile and chubby arms reaching toward me, I feel her love, and my heart overflows. Yet I know the love we share is incomplete without You. You are the author of this great blessing, and the closer we become to You, the more our love will abound. What joy that is!

✧ Rebekah Loved Jacob ✧

And Isaac loved Esau, because he did eat
of his venison: but Rebekah loved Jacob.
GENESIS 25:28

Father, I'm tempted to look at the faults of Isaac and Rebekah and to say they shouldn't have been playing favorites, but what I also notice is Rebekah loved Jacob simply because he was her son. You love me as one of Your children. Thank You for that amazing privilege.

✧ Cheap Talk ✧

My little children, let us not love in word,
neither in tongue; but in deed and in truth.
1 JOHN 3:18

Father, there is no greater example of the saying "Actions speak louder than words" than where love is concerned. It should be obvious to the people around me that I love them by the way I treat them. Unfortunately, my tone of voice or lack of attention often conveys other messages. Forgive me, Lord. Give me the patience to show love to others.

↠ The Power of Love ↞

Hatred stirreth up strifes: but love covereth all sins.
PROVERBS 10:12

I know we live in a fallen world, Lord. Evil abounds, and hatred and prejudice come easily. But these are bitter attitudes that poison the soul. Loving the unlovely is much more difficult, but when love permeates my soul, it opens my eyes and helps me realize that the other person needs You. God, please help me to love all people.

CHAPTER 10

My Praise: The Power of an Overflowing Heart

∞

We are blessed to live in a geographically diverse land. From the coastlines to the mountains to the open plain, we can observe the majesty of our Creator. If you live where few lights adulterate the night sky, you should make it a point to go outside on a clear night and watch the stars. Consider all that is actually contained in those pinpoints of brightness.

God's greatness truly is beyond our comprehension. Maybe that's why so many people reject Him. They can't understand Him, and it's easier to believe all of creation got here by chance. When we're honest with ourselves, we must admit this universe had to have a wise and intelligent creator. This truth is hard to fathom, but what is even harder to grasp is that He made each of us unique, and He takes a special interest in each individual. Is it any wonder David said, "The heavens declare the glory of God; and the firmament sheweth his handywork" (Psalm 19:1)?

In Psalm 150, a beautiful psalm of praise, we are challenged, "Let everything that hath breath praise the LORD. Praise ye the LORD" (v. 6). Have you taken this command seriously? I think often we get so caught up in the busyness of our days that our talks with God are a brief thanks for the day and a list of what we want or need. We really don't think about the One we are addressing. We forget that we are bowing before the almighty, all-wise God of the universe. We should be offering a sacrifice of sincere praise and worship.

Maybe this seems somewhat awkward to you if you are not used to including praise in your prayers. Start by singing hymns of adoration. God won't mind if you're a bit off-key—He made your voice exactly the way He wanted to. He's more interested in the attitude behind the song. You also might consider keeping a praise journal. Fill it with all the wonderful things you know and learn about your Savior. Begin talking to God about what you write. Soon your worship will become more natural, and you won't be able to keep from praising God.

→ Creation Will Praise God ←

Sing, O heavens; and be joyful, O earth;
and break forth into singing, O mountains:
for the LORD hath comforted his people,
and will have mercy upon his afflicted.
ISAIAH 49:13

I was made to praise You and Your great majesty, oh God. In fact, all creation—the heavens, the earth, the mountains—all Your works declare Your glory. Yet even in Your greatness You take time to offer comfort to Your people. Even with our imperfections You have mercy on us. You truly are a great God, worthy of infinitely more honor than I am capable of bestowing upon You.

⤞ Even at Midnight ⤝

And at midnight Paul and Silas prayed, and sang praises unto God: and the prisoners heard them.
ACTS 16:25

⤞ In Him Is Victory ⤝

I will call on the LORD, who is worthy to be praised: so shall I be saved from mine enemies.
2 SAMUEL 22:4

Lord, You are worthy of all my adoration. I'm amazed at how much I am blessed when I praise You. When I'm glorifying You, I feel Your strength. I know You are with me in a special way. I want my entire existence to be centered on You, for You are awesome. Without You my life would lie in shattered ruins, but You give me victory.

⇥ Thou Art Exalted ⇤

*Thine, O LORD is the greatness, and the power, and
the glory, and the victory, and the majesty: for all that
is in the heaven and in the earth is thine; thine is
the kingdom, O LORD, and thou art exalted as head
above all. Both riches and honour come of thee, and
thou reignest over all; and in thine hand is power and
might; and in thine hand it is to make great, and to
give strength unto all. Now therefore, our God,
we thank thee, and praise thy glorious name.*

1 CHRONICLES 29:11–13

⇥ Walking with God ⇤

*The fear of the LORD is the beginning of wisdom:
a good understanding have all they that do his
commandments: his praise endureth for ever.*

PSALM 111:10

Father, I've tried to teach my children that there is
good fear and bad fear. Please help them to understand that fearing You is the first step in walking
with You. As their respect for You grows, they will
want to know more about You and will choose to
obey You. As they obey You, they will get to know
You and adore You more fully. They will begin to
praise You fervently.

✦ The Heavenly Choir ✦

And they sing the song of Moses the servant of God,
and the song of the Lamb, saying, Great and
marvellous are thy works, Lord God Almighty;
just and true are thy ways, thou King of saints.
REVELATION 15:3

We sat amazed as the young people in our church sang, "Great and marvelous are thy works, Lord God Almighty." They sang with deep joy and sincerity. I began to think about how that same song will be even more beautiful when we hear it in the perfection of heaven. Lord, how truly wonderful You are!

✦ Meaningful Routine ✦

And to stand every morning to thank and praise
the LORD, and likewise at even.
1 CHRONICLES 23:30

Lord, You must have known we would need order, because You've told us what to include in our daily routine. Each morning we need to begin by praising You. We're also to end the day by praising You. Doing so helps us to recall Your blessings and greatness. Praising You gives us the right perspective.

✦ With My Whole Heart ✦

I will praise thee, O LORD, with my whole heart;
I will shew forth all thy marvellous works. I will be
glad and rejoice in thee: I will sing praise to thy name,
O thou most High. When mine enemies are turned
back, they shall fall and perish at thy presence.
For thou hast maintained my right and my cause;
thou satest in the throne judging right.

PSALM 9:1–4

✦ The Stones Would Cry Out ✦

And he answered and said unto them, I tell you that,
if these should hold their peace, the stones
would immediately cry out.

LUKE 19:40

In many instances adults aren't allowed to mention You in the workplace. Many public schools forbid public prayer. I would love to be there when the stones begin to sing Your praises. I would love to witness the reactions of those who made these wicked rules. Even better, though, would be the joy of seeing those who once rejected You come to know You and begin to join in the chorus glorifying You.

⇥ All Ye People ⇤

And again, Praise the Lord, all ye Gentiles;
and laud him, all ye people.
ROMANS 15:11

Thank You, Lord, that all people are important to You. Thank You that even I am instructed to praise You. You've done so much for me every day of my life. You give me strength and breath. You meet all my needs abundantly. The list goes on and on and is topped by the gift of Your precious Son. I cannot help but praise You.

⇥ The Marriage of the Lamb ⇤

And I saw an angel standing in the sun; and he
cried with a loud voice, saying to all the fowls that fly
in the midst of heaven, Come and gather yourselves
together unto the supper of the great God.
REVELATION 19:17

I've attended or participated in more weddings than I can count. Mostly they've been happy occasions, but my own was my favorite. Even that can't compare to the rejoicing that will take place the day You and Your bride are joined. I look forward to rejoicing with so many others the day that celebration takes place. I only ask that my children and loved ones will be there to join in on that glorious day.

❖ All My Days ❖

While I live will I praise the LORD:
I will sing praises unto my God
while I have any being.
PSALM 146:2

Each day You give me is a gift from You. I cannot help but praise You. Each breath is a blessing that must be taken in Your honor. The life I live should be a testament to Your greatness. My children, neighbors, and everyone I meet should be able to tell I've been walking with You. Lord, while I live and breathe, I will praise You.

❖ Thou Art Lord Alone ❖

Stand up and bless the LORD your God for ever
and ever: and blessed be thy glorious name,
which is exalted above all blessing and praise.
Thou, even thou, art LORD alone; thou hast made
heaven, the heaven of heavens, with all their host,
the earth, and all things that are therein, the seas,
and all that is therein, and thou preservest them all;
and the host of heaven worshippeth thee.
NEHEMIAH 9:5–6

CHAPTER 11

My Church: The Power of Christian Fellowship

∞

Ask many people to picture the word *church*, and they'll envision a building with a steeple. To them, a church is a place to conduct a worship service. Yet the church isn't simply a building, nor is a worship service limited to activities inside a structure.

The word *church* isn't found in the Old Testament. Jesus uses the word for the first time in the New Testament. He speaks of the church with a very specific meaning. The church is the body of believers. He uses several examples to describe His relationship to the church. He says He is the vine and His followers are the branches (see John 15). He also refers to the church as His body. These images show how closely believers are joined with Him and with one another. Romans 12:5 says, "So in Christ we, though many, form one body, and each member belongs to all the others" (NIV). Jesus is the head of the church.

The church refers to all of those people worldwide who have accepted Jesus as their Savior. Often, however, the word also means a group of local individuals who meet regularly to worship God. In either case, the church is a body of Christians who are in fellowship with Jesus and with one another. The first record of a church service is found in Acts 2:42: "They devoted themselves to the apostles' teaching and to fellowship, to the breaking of bread and to prayer" (NIV). God created the church to have an impact on both the believers and their communities. In this assembly we are encouraged to improve our service to the Lord. Singing, praying, studying the Bible, and engaging in other Christian activities are ways to worship God. At the same time, these activities strengthen our faith and refresh us in our determination to lead holy lives.

Sometimes we think of the worship service as requiring our attendance, and we walk away from it believing we've done our duty for the week. But worship extends beyond the weekly assembly. Offering a friendly smile, exercising patience in trying times, and giving an even-tempered reply to harsh words are as much acts of worship as are singing songs and listening to the Gospel.

The assembly of believers takes on additional importance when we think of it as a training ground that prepares us to enter the world and bring Jesus to those who are without Him. The institutions built by humans—governments, schools, businesses, organizations, and societies—attempt to solve the world's problems. But without the application of Christian principles, they have limited success. To the community, the church exemplifies the blessings that come from being in fellowship with Jesus.

To bring light to our neighbors, we need our spirits to be habitually renewed. Regular meetings with other Christians afford the opportunity to experience such renewal. The Bible reinforces the importance of meeting with other believers in Hebrews 10:25: "Let us. . .not give up meeting together, as some are in the habit of doing, but encouraging one another—and all the more as you see the Day approaching" (NIV).

✦ Body of Christ ✦

Although I am less than the least of all the Lord's people, this grace was given me: to preach to the Gentiles the boundless riches of Christ, and to make plain to everyone the administration of this mystery, which for ages past was kept hidden in God, who created all things. His intent was that now, through the church, the manifold wisdom of God should be made known to the rulers and authorities in the heavenly realms, according to his eternal purpose which he accomplished in Christ Jesus our Lord.
EPHESIANS 3:8–11 NIV

⚜ Love for the Church ⚜

Lord, I appreciate Your love for the church. You make Yourself known to us through the fellowship of believers. We are the works of Your hands, and our best attributes are a mirror of Your qualities. When we come together, help us reinforce those characteristics that best reveal Your nature. You are our ultimate model, but seeing others reflect Your love strengthens us, as well. I pray I will reflect the light of Your love.

⚜ Respect for Others ⚜

Lord, help me radiate a warm acceptance of fellow Christians. May they delight in meeting with me. Never should they feel that I'm examining their words or actions for hidden motives. Let my attitude show respect for their opinions and their service to You. May others leave my presence feeling that they have become more solid in their walk with You. I would be pleased if they become better people because they have known me.

✦ Image of Christ ✦

Lord, help me cultivate a strong bond with other church members. Guide me in developing confidence in them. Help me be reliable so that they, too, have confidence in me. It's vital that we act with one spirit and one purpose. Should we become cold toward one another, assist me in being the first to recognize the peril and to work to restore fellowship before unity is lost. Keep me focused not on myself but on You so that Christian love prevails.

✦ Honor for Leaders ✦

Dear Father, a person is honored to be a Christian and doubly honored to be a Christian leader. Blessed is the church that has loyal leaders who honestly seek after the truth. With the encouragement of their followers, they can concentrate on keeping their eyes fixed on You; we become a congregation with one spirit and one purpose. They need my support. They are due my respect. Give me the humility to accept and embrace their leadership.

✦ Christian Fellowship ✦

Father, I enjoy the fellowship of Christians. They believe in me and influence me to do better. In a world of suspicion and ulterior motives, it's a welcome relief to be in the company of those who choose to see me in the best light. They accept the sincerity of my purpose without bias. I'm refreshed in their presence. I pray I will honor Your church by enhancing their strengths rather than dwelling on their weaknesses.

✦ Senseless Criticism ✦

Lord, the church must do Your work, yet every action is an opportunity for criticism. I find flaws far too easily. I can argue with others about simple matters. Even successful efforts can be criticized because they are not outstanding enough. Turn me away from expressing disapproval that serves no purpose. Teach me to appreciate what others do. Develop in me the resolve to replace words that lead to disharmony with dialogue that supports unity.

⁑ The Church's Prayer for Boldness ⁕

*When they heard this, they raised their voices together
in prayer to God. "Sovereign Lord," they said,
"you made the heavens and the earth and the sea,
and everything in them. You spoke by the
Holy Spirit through the mouth of your servant,
our father David 'Why do the nations rage
and the peoples plot in vain? The kings of the
earth rise up and the rulers band together against
the Lord and against his anointed one.' "*

ACTS 4:24–26 NIV

⁑ Freedom to Worship ⁕

Heavenly Father, elsewhere in the world today, Christians face danger merely because they believe in You. To assemble as a church requires courage. I'm so blessed to gather with other Christians in freedom. Meeting with others to worship rekindles my spirit. Father, I desire to take the freedom of worshipping You beyond the church meeting place. Help me extend my faith and infuse my everyday life with service to You.

❖ Choosing the Best Course ❖

Lord, effective Christian action grows in an atmosphere of encouragement. In our work, many questions arise, such as which programs to support and how best to direct our efforts. I pray Your grace will be with all those in my church. Steer us along the best course between the rocks of hard-line fanaticism and the murky waters of caution. May we work as an agreeable team to bring honor to Your name.

❖ Jesus' Prayer for His Disciples ❖

*"They were yours; you gave them to me and
they have obeyed your word. Now they know
that everything you have given me comes from you.
For I gave them the words you gave me and they
accepted them. They knew with certainty that I came
from you, and they believed that you sent me.
I pray for them. I am not praying for the world,
but for those you have given me, for they are yours."*
JOHN 17:6–9 NIV

⋆ Others Help Me ⋆

Heavenly Father, help me keep my zeal for serving You. I will do my part by walking and talking with You. But when I'm low, bring into my life Christians with the gift of encouragement. Their encouragement will renew me, strengthen me, and put me on the right path. To receive the blessings that You provide through others, I must associate with other believers. Keep me faithful in regular church attendance.

⋆ I Help Others ⋆

Lord, You sacrificed for Your church. I, too, should put others before myself. I often need encouragement and welcome the embrace of fellow Christians. Similarly, help me be sensitive to others who have become dejected. Let me recognize those who are hurting and identify how I can represent You to help mend their spirits. Give me a ready response with the right words, actions, or examples to brighten their day. I pray they leave my presence with their joy increased.

☙ Focus ❧

Father, without You to guide us, we don't act as one. Instead, we are like a covey of quail winging away in all possible directions when disturbed; we encounter a sudden burst of uncoordinated action. Constant agitation keeps us from concentrating on the essential aims of the church. Our energy is dissipated. Lord, help us find common ground, guided by the Holy Spirit. I pray we will always submit our own wills to Yours.

☙ Wide Awake ❧

Father God, many aspects of my life are so routine that I can do them with only slight conscious effort. For my commute to work, I must guard against going on autopilot. Otherwise, an accident could result. More serious are those times when I've let my mind go into suspended animation during worship. Help me be wise enough not to deprive myself of Your presence. Build in me an upright heart that is fully awake to all of the benefits of worshipping You.

❖ Honing My Abilities ❖

Lord, I want to use my talents in service to my local congregation. I admire the abilities of those chosen to serve. Often, I compare myself unfavorably with them. Yet I know You have given me unique abilities. It's my duty to identify those special skills, hone them, and put them to use in the work of the church. Lord, with Your help I will give all I have in serving You.

CHAPTER 12

My Fulfillment: The Power of Accepting God's Plan

∞

In any person's life, the time comes when the question arises that demands an answer: Is this all there is? Even when a man has everything, the feeling persists that he's missing something. "I have a feeling this isn't all there is to life, is it?" Without an answer to the question, life has no peace and no purpose. If a man consciously looks away to pretend the question doesn't exist, his life becomes hollow. Only by attending to the question, by accepting that God exists and that He has a plan for us, can we discover fulfillment.

Knowing Christ is the only path to true fulfillment. All others lead to emptiness. By accepting Christ, by living in the will of God, we find satisfaction. The Bible often tells of people who recognized that God had a purpose for them: Paul (2 Timothy 3:10), David (Psalm 138:8), and others. The Bible says, " 'For I know the plans I have for you,' declares the LORD, 'plans to prosper you and not to harm you, plans to give you hope and a future'" (Jeremiah 29:11 NIV).

But when I became a Christian, the hollowness didn't entirely go away. I wanted to have a truly significant impact on my family and even the world. However, I thought I was wise enough to know what God intended for me. I pursued my own goals, but that led to emptiness. I recognized I needed to grow, but I focused on myself. The fulfillment was hollow. I needed not to concentrate on myself, but to center myself on God for Him to reveal His purpose for me. Pursuing God's goals leads to fulfillment.

God wants my heart more than any works I might do. To find fulfillment, I first must grow a satisfying relationship with God. Then I can see the difference between serving myself and serving God. When I'm no longer preoccupied with my own fulfillment, I can see more clearly those opportunities that God provides. My fulfillment comes from reaching goals put before me by Jesus rather than goals I set for myself.

Are you seeking fulfillment? Then immediately begin doing what you can with what you have rather than wishing for more. You need not be overly concerned about your current limitations. God said to Israel, "So do not fear, for I am with you; do not be dismayed, for I am your God. I will strengthen you and help you; I will uphold you with my righteous right hand" (Isaiah 41:10 NIV).

God offers many opportunities to do good: defending the cause of the weak and fatherless and maintaining the rights of the poor and oppressed (Psalm 82:3), binding up the brokenhearted (Isaiah 61:1), visiting the sick and captive (Matthew 25:39), and bringing salvation to the lost (Matthew 28:19). The grace of Jesus, the love of God, and the guidance of the Holy Spirit will direct you to a special cause that will bring true fulfillment.

✣ Prayer for Fulfillment ✣

Have mercy on me, my God, have mercy on me,
for in you I take refuge. I will take refuge in
the shadow of your wings until the disaster has passed.
I cry out to God Most High, to God, who
vindicates me. He sends from heaven and saves me,
rebuking those who hotly pursue me—
God sends forth his love and his faithfulness.
PSALM 57:1–3 NIV

✣ Mission for the Lord ✣

Lord, I know You have a work for me. You shine Your light on me and illuminate the path that will lead to my destiny. When I understand my special mission, I pray I will accept it and not stop short. May I seize it with wholehearted determination.

Lord, with Your strength, I will follow through to its successful completion. I offer thanksgiving and praise that I can be of service to You.

→ *Emptiness* ←

Lord, when I go into an empty room, I turn on the lights. If I must wait in the room for a while, I will pick up something to read or turn on music or the television. I can't long endure darkness or silence. Lord, when I have emptiness in my life, I rush to fill the void. I will come to You in prayer to fill my life with joy, love, kindness, and the other fruits of the Spirit.

→ *Volunteering* ←

Lord, You gave Paul the opportunity to mention one of the statements of Jesus that isn't found anywhere in the Gospels: "It is more blessed to give than to receive" (Acts 20:35 NIV). When I spend some time in volunteer work, I always end the session feeling better than when I began. Occasionally, I can do the volunteer effort with my family. We are brought closer together through the shared experience. Thank You for giving me the opportunity to serve others and bring fulfillment to us.

✦ Solomon's Prayer for Wisdom ✦

*Solomon answered, "You have shown great kindness
to your servant, my father David, because he was
faithful to you and righteous and upright in heart. You
have continued this great kindness to him and have
given him a son to sit on his throne this very day. . . .
So give your servant a discerning heart to govern your
people and to distinguish between right and wrong.
For who is able to govern this great people of yours?"*
1 KINGS 3:6, 9 NIV

✦ Renewal ✦

Lord Jesus, I'm often in need of renewal. Anxiety, discouragement, and physical and spiritual exhaustion take their toll. I know You prayed for others, but You also prayed for Yourself. I now come before You and humbly ask You to attend to my special needs. Lord, these personal requests benefit only me. Provided they are in Your will, I ask that they be granted.

✦ Capacity ✦

Lord, I showed my son a glass filled to the midpoint with water. I asked him what he saw, thinking he would give either the pessimistic answer of half empty or the optimistic answer of half full. Instead, he said the glass was too big for its contents. Lord, I realize my expectations can exceed my capacity. I pray I will understand that fulfillment comes from doing what I can with what I have rather than wishing for more.

✦ Motivation ✦

Lord, as my school and college career progressed, I discovered that someone always rose to be better than me in any particular subject. Lord, I'm thankful You don't measure me by the abilities of others. You use me whether I'm at the top of the class or struggling to pass. But I must strive to rise to the ability You have given me. Thank You for measuring my value by my willingness to serve You.

✦ Throne of Honor ✦

*Then Hannah prayed and said: "My heart rejoices
in the LORD; in the LORD my horn is lifted high.
My mouth boasts over my enemies, for I delight in
your deliverance. . . . The LORD sends poverty and
wealth; he humbles and he exalts. He raises the poor
from the dust and lifts the needy from the ash heap;
he seats them with princes and has them inherit a
throne of honor. For the foundations of the earth
are the Lord's; upon them he has set the world."*

1 SAMUEL 2:1, 7–8 NIV

✦ Latent Energy ✦

Lord, when I studied physics, I learned about latent
energy—hidden energy that could be brought out
under the right circumstances. As Your special creation, I have the capacity for growth and development. Let me not be concerned about my current
limitations. Instead, help me work toward my hidden
promise. I ask You to bring out my full potential. I
want to be a tool in Your hands to achieve what I'm
capable of doing.

✦ Person of Distinction ✦

Lord, I know character can't be constructed in a moment. It must be built over a lifetime of making the right choices and taking the correct actions. Help me build my character with the building blocks of honesty, honor, helpfulness, and humility. I pray I will always be mindful of what builds my character and avoid those actions that tarnish it. May I succeed while maintaining my integrity.

✦ Seeing the Future ✦

Lord, I earnestly seek a faith determined to please You. You have guided me this far, and I pray I will accept Your plan for my life until I have fulfilled my destiny. I ask that You open my eyes to Your Word as specific guidance for me in particular. I have received daily blessings from You, and I desire to continue in the way that leads to the final blessing of being with You forever.

✦ Glorious Name ✦

*And the Levites. . .said: "Stand up and praise the
Lord your God, who is from everlasting to everlasting.
"Blessed be your glorious name, and may it be exalted
above all blessing and praise. You alone are the LORD.
You made the heavens, even the highest heavens, and
all their starry host, the earth and all that is on it, the
seas and all that is in them. You give life to everything,
and the multitudes of heaven worship you."*

NEHEMIAH 9:5–6 NIV

✦ Best Years ✦

Lord, on the street where my parents live, couples
whose children are grown occupy most homes.
Some of my parents' neighbors live in tight financial conditions. A few have medical conditions
that limit their activities. Others are of retirement
age but must work part-time jobs. Yet I see that
those who have embraced You view these years as
the best times of their lives. I'm learning that Your
peace is far more wonderful than I can understand.

✦ Top Off ✦

Lord, before my family and I leave on a long driving trip, I check the car. In addition to topping off all of the fluid levels, I replenish a small survival kit and check the air pressure in the spare. Lord, my life is a long journey. I need to replenish myself for the journey through prayer and meditation on Your Word. I ask that I complete the journey successfully and be welcomed into heaven, my final destination.

✦ Mold Me ✦

Lord, I'm fascinated with unfinished or incomplete works of art: Venus de Milo's missing arms, Gilbert Stuart's unfinished portrait of George Washington, and Beethoven's unfinished Tenth Symphony. Whether by accident, death, or intention, they represent the tension of a work left in limbo. Lord, I know I'm a work in progress, but I ask You to continue to shape me. I know You won't abandon me, and I'm willing to be clay that is molded in Your hands.

CHAPTER 13

My History: The Power of a Forgiven Past

❧

No two people are alike, and no two people have identical accounts of their lives before receiving the salvation of Jesus. Here are some sample cases, reduced to their essentials, that represent the variety. One young man's history followed a straight line. "I was born into a good Christian family. Dad and Mom had a huge influence on me. I accepted Christ at an early age and have walked with Him ever since."

Another man followed a similar path but with a variation. "I came to accept Christ at an early age, but during my teen and young adult years, I strayed away. I became a lukewarm Christian. I discarded my earlier teaching and fell into destructive dependencies on drugs. But through a series of events that I now see were the result of prayers by my Christian friends, I began once again walking with the Lord." Another man was exposed to religious teaching, but he never fully accepted the Gospel. Later, he met a Christian girlfriend and found her filled with joy and compassion. "I came to see God's endless love and accept Christianity as the path to happiness."

Another example: A thirty-eight-year-old man ignored others' attempts to tell him about Jesus. He lived a hard life, struggled to earn a living, and had brushes with the law. As he neared middle age, his wife was the only bright spot in his life. She stood by him despite his many failings. But his wife became desperately ill. He and his few family members gathered around her hospital bed. A visiting Christian suggested reading from the Bible. The Bible, open to John 14:1–3, was thrust into his hands. In a halting voice, he read, "Do not let your hearts be troubled. You believe in God; believe also in me. My Father's house has many rooms; if that were not so, would I have told you that I am going there to prepare a place for you? And if I go and prepare a place for you, I will come back and take you to be with me that you also may be where I am" (NIV). He never knew that the Bible could bring such comfort. Despite his age, despite his baggage of a life full of sin, he gave himself to Jesus.

Many individual accounts are mirrored by some of the churches that received letters written by the apostle John. "[Ephesus,] you have forsaken the love you had at first. Consider how far you have fallen! Repent and do the things you did at first" (Revelation 2:4–5 NIV). "So, because you [Laodicea] are lukewarm—neither hot nor cold—I am about to spit you out of my mouth" (Revelation 3:16 NIV).

Individuals can't change their past. But they can change their future. Past sins, lost opportunities, and lives lived in darkness are overwhelmed by the light of God's love. Salvation erases past offenses and replaces them with a new life. A Christian's true history begins on the day of salvation.

✦ Prayer for Seven Churches ✦

Grace and peace to you from him who is, and
who was, and who is to come, and from the seven
spirits before his throne, and from Jesus Christ,
who is the faithful witness, the firstborn from the dead,
and the ruler of the kings of the earth. To him who
loves us and has freed us from our sins by his blood,
and has made us to be a kingdom and priests
to serve his God and Father—to him be glory
and power for ever and ever! Amen.
REVELATION 1:4–6 NIV

✦ Successful Outcome ✦

Lord, in my past I had a poor opinion of myself. I never felt my best efforts were good enough. If something could be done two different ways, I usually felt I had chosen the way that took longer, looked worse, or cost more. I became cautious about taking on any new endeavor. Lord, I'm thankful You give me the confidence to try difficult assignments. When I rely on You and seek Your help, I will find the route to success.

→ Daily Training ←

Lord, I often think I deal with one minor predicament after another. But when a major crisis arises, I see that You have been preparing me for it. The little problems were opportunities for growth and prepared me for the major crisis. You are equipping me to succeed despite momentary setbacks. You can see the future and know what I must do to be ready for it. Thank You for strengthening me day by day.

→ Forgiven and Forgotten ←

Lord, an artist friend had a painting damaged by his daughter. Eventually, he forgave her and repaired the damage. But every time he looked at the painting, he remembered her careless action. He gave away the painting so he could fully forget what she had done. Lord, I know You have forgiven my earlier, careless life. You have cast aside all of my sins and no longer remember them. Thank You for Your forgiveness.

✢ Elijah's Prayer of Self-Pity ✦

*[Elijah] replied, "I have been very zealous for the
LORD God Almighty. The Israelites have rejected your
covenant, torn down your altars, and put your
prophets to death with the sword. I am the only one
left, and now they are trying to kill me too."... The
LORD said to him, ... "Yet I reserve seven thousand in
Israel—all whose knees have not bowed down to Baal
and all whose mouths have not kissed him."*
1 KINGS 19:10, 15, 18 NIV

✢ Do-Over ✦

Lord, my wife was explaining to one of our children
about repentance and forgiveness. When she asked if
he understood, he said, "Yes, it's like a do-over." Lord,
I'm thankful You give me the opportunity to start
fresh. Once I repent, You erase the errors behind me
and give me a clean page on which to write my future.

✢ Success Has Many Fathers ✦

Lord, according to a saying, "Success has many
fathers, but failure is an orphan." Looking back, I've
been too determined to distance myself from failure.
This determination has created adversaries, strained
partnerships, and broken friendships. Help me

understand that failure is merely a testing ground for maturity. By accepting responsibility for my actions and learning to control them, I'm being built as a stronger Christian. Help me learn and move forward.

✣ Breaking the Cycle ✣

Lord, my early history was one of repeated mistakes leading to the same bleak outcome. I did exactly the same action under identical circumstances and was surprised when I encountered the same unfortunate result. Lord, I know mistakes are part of my life, but I need to break the cycle of repeating them. I'm thankful that because I have accepted You, my mistakes have become lessons leading me to change. Please continue to lead me to a better life.

✣ Sins Confessed ✣

*"Now therefore, our God, the great God, mighty
and awesome, who keeps his covenant of love,
do not let all this hardship seem trifling in
your eyes—the hardship that has come on us,
on our kings and leaders, on our priests and
prophets, on our ancestors and all your people,
from the days of the kings of Assyria until today.
In all that has happened to us, you remained righteous;
you have acted faithfully, while we acted wickedly."*
NEHEMIAH 9:32–33 NIV

⇥ Two Men's Prayers ⇤

To some who were confident of their own righteousness
and looked down on everyone else, Jesus told this
parable: "Two men went up to the temple to pray,
one a Pharisee and the other a tax collector.
The Pharisee stood by himself and prayed:
'God, I thank you that I am not like other people—
robbers, evildoers, adulterers—or even like this
tax collector. I fast twice a week and
give a tenth of all I get.' "
LUKE 18:9–12 NIV

⇥ Image of God ⇤

Lord, while visiting the canyon country of the
American Southwest, I've seen how changes are
made to solid rock by the ever-present wind and
sudden cloudbursts. When I look at these impres-
sive stone monuments, I realize You have been
changing my life. Whether those alterations are
slow or sudden, gentle or forceful, subtle or obvious, I'm thankful I welcomed You into my life to
shape me into the person You want me to be.

❧ Gift Card ❧

Lord, You gave me the gift of life. I spent the first part of it without knowing its source. Like a gift card with no dollar limit, I recklessly used the time in selfish pursuits. Happily, before my time expired, I accepted Your saving grace. Now I arise each morning thankful that You have given me another day. I pray I will always be aware that each moment is a precious commodity. May I spend it wisely.

❧ David's Prayer of Repentance ❧

Have mercy on me, O God, according to your
unfailing love; according to your great compassion
blot out my transgressions. Wash away all my iniquity
and cleanse me from my sin. For I know my
transgressions, and my sin is always before me.
Against you, you only, have I sinned and done
what is evil in your sight, so you are right in
your verdict and justified when you judge.
PSALM 51:1–4 NIV

✦ Conversation ✦

Lord, sometimes I talk so much that others become weary of my stories. My children tell me they have heard my old jokes and my childhood memories too many times. When I'm lonely, I often talk on and on without saying anything important. Lord, thank You for the avenue of prayer that You provide for me to talk to You. You are never too busy to listen and to hear my prayers.

✦ Around and Around ✦

Lord, a pilot friend told me he became weary of repeatedly making takeoffs and landings during his training. But his instructor insisted on being thoroughly satisfied with his flying skills before letting him go solo. Lord, during my early development as a Christian, I sometimes wanted to move on to more important roles. But You trained me in easy, small steps. Thank You for keeping me in check until I developed Christian principles to Your satisfaction.

✢ Spiritually Depleted ✢

Lord, I can monitor my car's fuel situation with a fuel computer, a warning light, and a fuel gauge. Lord, during my early days, a multitude of signs warned me that my spiritual life was running on empty. I chose to ignore them for a time and continued on my destructive path. I'm thankful I heeded Your call to make a change. Keep me monitoring my life so I never run on empty again.

CHAPTER 14

My Future: The Power of Seeking Eternity

∞

Before becoming a Christian, I lived a present-day life, concerned mainly with ordinary, everyday affairs without giving much thought to the future. I couldn't understand the ultimate purpose of my existence. Because there appeared to be no answer, I seldom thought about the matter. I looked at eternity out of the corner of my eye and pretended it didn't exist.

I wasn't alone. Rather than being forward thinking, many people who haven't accepted Jesus live only for the present or even focus on the past. They tend to mull over past successes or past grievances and ponder how those events have affected their present circumstances. Thinking of the future would bring them face-to-face with the question of eternity, which they—and I, once—would prefer to avoid. When I accepted Jesus, eternity became something I sought rather than avoided. I became a forward-thinking person. I became more interested in the future and less interested in squandering my time in vain pursuits. I saw new meaning for my existence. Peter writes, "Praise be to the God and

Father of our Lord Jesus Christ! In his great mercy he has given us new birth into a living hope through the resurrection of Jesus Christ from the dead, and into an inheritance that can never perish, spoil or fade. This inheritance is kept in heaven for you" (1 Peter 1:3–4 NIV).

My life in Jesus began with a new birth, which gave me a new identity and a new vision that guided me. God lovingly sought a personal, eternal relationship with me. He numbered my days on earth as a time to prepare for eternity with Him. A new birth implied growth. Through prayer and Bible study, a persistent concept grew in my heart of the person God wanted me to be. I allowed God to prepare me for heaven.

Heaven is the eventual destination of Christians. When Jesus ascended into heaven, He went to prepare a place for His people. We are, in fact, already citizens of heaven. The Bible says, "But our citizenship is in heaven. And we eagerly await a Savior from there, the Lord Jesus Christ, who, by the power that enables him to bring everything under his control, will transform our lowly bodies so that they will be like his glorious body" (Philippians 3:20–21 NIV). Heaven gives meaning to our lives.

Often the first year after being born again is the most meaningful time for a new Christian. As the fire burns strongly, the new believer's mind seeks with a feverish intensity to become all that God intends him to be. As he grows and develops, he may tend to fall once again into the futile trap of reflecting on his life to see if he has made a difference. But none of us have the skills to judge how effective our lives have been. Paul says, "I planted the seed, Apollos watered it, but God has been making it grow" (1 Corinthians 3:6 NIV). A spiritual vision faces forward. Without undue concern for the past, we look to our future.

⇻ From Heaven ⇺

So I said: "Do not take me away, my God, in the midst of my days; your years go on through all generations. In the beginning you laid the foundations of the earth, and the heavens are the work of your hands. They will perish, but you remain; they will all wear out like a garment. Like clothing you will change them and they will be discarded. But you remain the same, and your years will never end. The children of your servants will live in your presence; their descendants will be established before you."
PSALM 102:24–28 NIV

⇻ Joy in Heaven ⇺

Heavenly Father, at the end of the day when I pick up my small child at preschool, he is happy as he plays with a toy. When he sees me, he swoops over to be swung overhead as I pick him up. His face reveals more than happiness. He is joyful because he is in the arms of his father. Lord, how joyful must be the event when we come home to You and You pick us up and we share our joy with each other.

✦ Pure Life ✦

Father, You have given me a recipe for success. When I try to mix secular concepts with biblical principles, the result will be an unacceptable mishmash. Keep me from the naive belief that I can improve on Your Word. Instead, let me live a pure life based firmly on the Gospel. When my life draws to a close, I want to see a future untainted by false premises.

✦ Brighter Future ✦

Lord, because I have followed the light of Your Word, You have carried me through adversity, comforted me in times of distress, and positioned me to receive success. With Your guiding light, my future has always looked brighter than my past. I ask that all aspects of my life reflect Your love to others. No matter what happens, I will remain triumphant because of Your gift of eternal life.

➤ Jesus' Prayer for Believers to Join Him in Heaven ➤

"Father, I want those you have given me to be with me where I am, and to see my glory, the glory you have given me because you loved me before the creation of the world. Righteous Father, though the world does not know you, I know you, and they know that you have sent me. I have made you known to them, and will continue to make you known in order that the love you have for me may be in them and that I myself may be in them."

JOHN 17:24–26 NIV

➤ In God We Trust ➤

Lord, in my country, "In God we trust" is the national motto. The words appear on all of our coins and paper money. However, the motto can be an empty sentiment, or it can be a guiding principle. Lord, I desire that my trust in You take on real meaning. I want trust in You to be an action word in my life. Even when the future is obscured, I will walk beside You knowing that You are leading me in the right way.

✦ Future Prospects ✦

Heavenly Father, with Your blessings I have learned to live and even thrive in this world. Sometimes I become satisfied with my circumstances. Then unexpected misfortune awakens me to the fact that things can go wrong very quickly. Help me always be aware that the earth is not my final destination. The earth is a testing ground to prepare me for eternity with You. Lord, keep my eyes not on my present circumstances but on my future prospects.

✦ Beyond the Event Horizon ✦

Jesus, I'm fascinated by what physicists describe as the event horizon around a black hole. Gravity becomes so overwhelming that even light can't escape. Physicists don't understand what lies beyond the event horizon. Lord, earlier in my life, the concept of eternal life was beyond comprehension. Although I still don't fully understand what awaits me, I know You have conquered death. Thank You for giving me eternal life with You.

✧ Prayer of Worship in Heaven ✧

The twenty-four elders, who were seated on their thrones before God, fell on their faces and worshiped God, saying: "We give thanks to you, Lord God Almighty, the One who is and who was, because you have taken your great power and have begun to reign."
REVELATION 11:16–17 NIV

✧ Future Trust ✧

Guiding Father, when walking in nature preserves, I carry a trail guide. It reassures me that I'll reach a destination that may not be readily visible. My spiritual travels are similar. I live in the present but wish to see the eternal. My faith is too frail to see beyond the present. Lord, build my trust to accept what is to come. I put everything in Your hands. Give me the mind to believe the fact that my trust will carry into a future reality.

✧ Heavenly Thanksgiving ✧

Lord, each year at Thanksgiving, we have a large family gathering. Each year, I remember with sadness those who have met the end of their mortal lives. Still, the number present remains relatively constant. A child is born, a son or daughter takes a spouse, or a relative from a distant city manages to come. Lord, I look forward to an everlasting reunion with You in Your heavenly kingdom.

→ See and Avoid ←

Lord, numerous accidental collisions on a lake caused the water patrol to launch a "See and be seen" program. When the program failed to reduce boating accidents, the water patrol changed the motto to "See and avoid." Under the first program, strong-willed individuals at the helm assumed the other fellow would change course. Lord, I know seeing and recognizing sin isn't enough. I need to avoid it, as well. Remind me to change course when my direction is leading me toward spiritual disaster.

→ Praying by the Crystal Sea ←

I saw what looked like a sea of glass glowing with fire and, standing beside the sea, those who had been victorious over the beast. . . . [They sang] the song. . . of the Lamb: "Great and marvelous are your deeds, Lord God Almighty. Just and true are your ways, King of the nations. Who will not fear you, Lord, and bring glory to your name? For you alone are holy. All nations will come and worship before you, for your righteous acts have been revealed."
REVELATION 15:2–4 NIV

✦ Final Chapter ✦

Lord, I read mystery stories and enjoy the suspense of learning "who done it" in the final chapter. But in real life, I don't enjoy suspense. Reading Revelation is special to me. Although I don't understand the entire book, it clearly reveals that a victorious Jesus locks Satan away for all time. I can live my life certain of a glorious resurrection and an eternity in a heavenly home with You.

✦ Vast Unknown ✦

Father, as I put aside my pen to meditate, an insect as small as a pinpoint began to trek across the white page. From his vantage point, the world beyond the edge of the sheet was a vast unknown. It was probably incomprehensible to his bug brain. Lord, I, too, am limited in what I can see and understand. But despite my limitations, I accept Your Word and believe that a better place is waiting for me.

⇥ *Different World Tomorrow* ⇤

Heavenly Father, my world will be different tomorrow because of the choices I make today. Guide me to the proper decisions that will prepare me for an eternal life with You. Lord, I understand my actions can influence the lives of others and make a different future for them. Help me choose to participate in supplying my resources by setting others on the heavenly way.

CHAPTER 15

My Identity: The Power of Who I Am in Christ

∞

One recent graduate, who had not yet decided if she was ready to hit the job market, prepared for the onslaught of questions for back-to-school night at her daughter's elementary school. She had cleverly ordered business cards that read: JULIE STOUT, DOMESTIC ENGINEER, with her home phone and address, cell phone, and e-mail address.

The way we think of ourselves has everything to do with how the world sees us. When you look in the mirror, you see a graduate—but what kind of graduate? Are you confident, shy, easily intimidated, or ready to take on the world? *Graduate* doesn't really tell the world who you are, but it does say that you are transitioning to the next step in your life.

When you meet someone, the first question you're asked after your name is, "What do you do?" We define each other by what we *do* rather than who we *are*. Often our occupations instead of our commitment to Christ define us to others.

Jesus asked His disciples, "Who do people say I am?" The disciples replied from various people's perspectives, "Some say John the Baptist; others say, Elijah; and still others, one of the prophets." Then Jesus pointed the question at them, "But what about you?" Peter answered, "You are the Messiah" (Mark 8:27–29 NIV).

Peter recognized Jesus because the Holy Spirit revealed who He was. Through the Holy Spirit's revelation, the disciples saw God when they saw Jesus. He said and did what the Father told Him to do and say. He lived in the power of His heavenly Father's will, consistent with His Father's character.

At some point in your life you were probably introduced to someone based on your relationship with someone else—Annie's sister, Professor Vance's student, or Rich's friend. Now, imagine if you were introduced to others based on your relationship with God. *This is God's child, Stephen. He's the spitting image of his heavenly Father—so strong and courageous.* Or, *C'mon over and meet Shelley, she's so compassionate, just like Christ!*

As a Christian, your relationship with God should be the foundation of your identity. The only way to find out who you are and who you are meant to be is to discover God's identity and the character that goes along with it.

Ephesians 5:1 says, "Follow God's example, therefore, as dearly loved children" (NIV).

Throughout the Bible you read of who God is and how He relates to you. You can find your own identity within the pages that describe His character,

His morals, His values, His work ethic—His identity. As you spend time in prayer with Him, you will experience His presence and a personal relationship with Him, and you will grow in His likeness.

The amazing power of who you are in Christ provides you with everything you need to succeed. When you are weak, He is strong. He has made you more than a conqueror, an overcomer in this life. No matter what battles you face, you can do all things through Christ who gives you strength.

✦ I Am God's Child ✦

The Spirit of God, who raised Jesus
from the dead, lives in you.
ROMANS 8:11 NLT

Jesus, thank You for providing the way for me to belong to Your family. Everyone who accepts You and believes in You becomes a child of God. I am born of God—not from natural birth, but spiritual birth. You are my example, and I will do my best to follow in Your footsteps. I want to be like You and our heavenly Father. I want to have the same character and nature. I receive Your gift of inclusion in the greatest family of all eternity.

✦ God's Definition ✦

When I meet new people, they always ask me what I do. Then I feel as though they're judging me as to whether I should be remembered. It's hard *not* to allow what I do to define me. Help me remember that my education and profession don't define me. Even who my parents are and where I grew up or went to school have nothing to do with who You created me to be. You are the Creator and, therefore, You define me. You make me who I am created to be. I am Your child, committed to living a life as genuine and true to Your purpose and plan as I can.

✦ A Matter of Significance ✦

To them God willed to make known what are the riches of the glory of this mystery among the Gentiles: which is Christ in you, the hope of glory.
COLOSSIANS 1:27 NKJV

Jesus, help me to find my identity in You. I know that my relationship with You is significant. As I read the Bible, give me an understanding of who You created me to be. Point out the true identity that has been given to me through the gift of salvation and my relationship with You.

❖ Facing the Truth ❖

The spirit of a man is the lamp of the LORD,
searching all the inner depths of his heart.
PROVERBS 20:27 NKJV

Lord, I know I need to change a lot of things in
my life. Thank You for accepting me as I am, where
I am today. You see the potential of who I can be,
even when I can't see it. Show me the things in my
heart that You want to change. Open my eyes; I
don't want to pretend anymore. Help me see the
truth so You can make me new!

❖ A Vote of Confidence ❖

I don't want to pretend to be someone I'm not. Help
me to stand up to the pressure that others place
on me to conform. Lord, You are my confidence!
I can do all things through Jesus Christ who gives
me strength to face today's challenges—even when
those challenges are people. Give me the words
to stay true to my commitment to You. I remind
myself of all the things that You have done, all the
battles You have fought on my behalf. With You at
my side and in my heart, I know I can succeed.

✦ An Imitator of God ✦

*Everyone who believes that Jesus is the Christ
has become a child of God.*
1 JOHN 5:1 NLT

Father, my relationship with You affects my personality in amazing ways. Many people have a negative idea of what it means to be a Christian. Forgive me when I've failed to be like You. I want to be so full of Your presence that others see You in everything I say and do. I never want anything I do to reflect negatively on You. I want to be like Jesus, of whom people said, "This truly was the Son of God!"

✦ Finding Courage ✦

Jesus, thank You for the courage to live my life following Your example. I can do all things through You who gives me the power to succeed. I refuse to be intimidated by what others say, think, or do. I live my life according to our Father's will and the Holy Spirit's instruction. Help me to declare to others the freedom I have found in You, so I point the way to You. Equip me to lead others to follow You.

✦ Finding Assurance ✦

I have been crucified with Christ and
I no longer live, but Christ lives in me.
The life I now live in the body,
I live by faith in the Son of God,
who loved me and gave himself for me.
GALATIANS 2:20 NIV

When people see me, let them see You. Help me not to confuse who You say I am with self-confidence, arrogance, or pride. My confidence is only because You live in and through me. Give me wisdom to know when to speak and when to listen so others may know You through my actions.

✦ Living without Guilt or Shame ✦

I have a list of things that make me feel guilty. They shout at me. I've told You my sins, and You have forgiven me, but I remember. Lord, help me to let go of my past mistakes. Help me to forgive myself. These things are like heavy chains keeping me from living the life of freedom that comes from a relationship with You. Today, I lift them off my shoulders and leave them at Your feet. Help me to never pick them up again. I let them go now. I am free today in Jesus' name!

❖ *Life from a Positive Perspective* ❖

But you are a chosen people, a royal priesthood,
a holy nation, God's special possession, that
you may declare the praises of him who called
you out of darkness into his wonderful light.
1 PETER 2:9 NIV

As I learn who I am in Christ, I realize that I need to look at life from a positive perspective. My life in You is not about what I'm missing or don't have. It's about Your light and life working in and through me. In even the most difficult situations I will find Your goodness in me.

❖ *Nothing Missing—Complete* ❖

I always felt I was missing something in my life before I met You. You are the missing piece of the puzzle. Now, no matter what I face, I know that I lack no good thing. When I am weak, You are strong. Instead of discouragement, I have boldness to do the things that without You I couldn't do. When life is a mess, You comfort me with Your peace. With You in my life, I am complete. All I need is You—nothing else.

☩ To Live in Christ ☩

*Anyone who belongs to Christ has become
a new person. The old life is gone;
a new life has begun!*
2 CORINTHIANS 5:17 NLT

In Your love and mercy You gave me life when You raised Christ from the dead. I was lost and alone, but You found me. You picked me up and gave me all the benefits of Your own Son, Jesus. Thank You for Your incredible kindness. All I had to do was believe and receive this gift. I can't take credit for it—it was all You! Father, continue to make me new each day in Christ.

☩ To Be a Peacemaker ☩

Jesus, You said, "Blessed are the peacemakers, for they will be called children of God" (Matthew 5:9 NIV). I want to be a peacemaker because it brings me closer to You. Help me to be open to other points of view and to think before I talk. Show me Your plan of peace in difficult situations. Remind me that it's more important to let others see You in me than to prove to them that I am right. When there doesn't seem to be a peaceful solution, show me Your way to peace.

⤳ Let Love Rule ⤳

"Live out your God-created identity.
Live generously and graciously toward others,
the way God lives toward you."
MATTHEW 5:48 MSG

Lord, help me to get rid of anger, cruelty, slander, and dirty language. I have the mind of Christ and can exercise self-control. Show me how to live my life with mercy, kindness, humility, gentleness, and patience. Remind me to allow for others' faults, even when they don't allow for mine. I want to be quick to forgive. Above all, help me to let Christ govern my heart. Please forgive me when I forget and take control.

CHAPTER 16

My Attitude: The Power of My Thoughts

∞

Positive thoughts are one key to a great attitude. Beating yourself up with thoughts that you'll never be good enough, that you don't deserve to be loved, and that you aren't smart enough will ultimately steal your dream—not to mention take the joy out of your life. It's hard to maintain a great attitude when your thinking is negative. But when you believe what God says about you and your circumstances, then you build something beautiful in your heart and mind.

Don't think that positive thinking is enough—it takes faith to rely on God to bring change to your heart and mind. Past experiences have shaped your attitudes and values about the world around you. The apostle Paul challenges us to "not be conformed to this world, but be transformed by the renewing of your mind, that you may prove what is that good and acceptable and perfect will of God" (Romans 12:2 NKJV).

Somewhere along the life-road you've walked, someone has done something to hurt you. Maybe it wasn't even intentional, but you wanted to see them punished for what they did. You most likely wanted to lash out or pay them back. But God's Word clearly tells you to forgive that person. Depending on how hurt you were, you probably needed some time to sort it all out. Your attitude about that person probably stunk for a while.

God's desire is for you to forgive that person—allow that to sink in and change your thoughts, and eventually you can choose to truly forgive them through your trust in God. It could mean thinking more about God's love and your desire to do His will, rather than thinking about what that person did to you.

The Bible is clear in what we should be thinking about. "Finally, brethren, whatever things are true, whatever things are noble, whatever things are just, whatever things are pure, whatever things are lovely, whatever things are of good report, if there is any virtue and if there is anything praiseworthy—meditate on these things" (Philippians 4:8 NKJV). The truth may be that the person hurt you, but thinking about that situation isn't lovely or a good report.

When you're tempted to think thoughts that contradict who you are in Christ, counteract them with thoughts about how important you are to God. Take the time to pray and ask God to encourage you. Spending time with Him and thinking about how much He loves you can turn your attitude around. Recount to the Lord all the wonderful things He's done for you. Picture yourself doing the things God put you on the earth to do. Choose your thoughts—change your life!

✦ For a More Positive Attitude ✦

Lord, You look into my heart and see the truth of how I think and feel. I won't pretend anymore, because I know I can be real with You. Help me to let go of the things that have hurt and angered me. I don't want those things to be my focus. I want to be focused on You and what You have planned for my life today. Help me to do what I need to do without grumbling, complaining, or pointing fingers at others. Fill me with Your joy and strengthen me with Your love.

✦ Gaining Control of My Thoughts ✦

"For the LORD searches all hearts and understands all the intent of the thoughts."
1 CHRONICLES 28:9 NKJV

Sometimes I feel like my thoughts are carrying on a conversation and I'm just observing. I feel out of control. But then I remember that You know me better than I know myself. I remember I have control over my thoughts. I turn them toward You and concentrate on what Your Word says about me. I have the mind of Christ. He lived His life saying and doing what You told Him to say and do—and I can, too.

✦ Transforming My Thoughts ✦

Father, Your Word says I can choose what to think about. Help me to refuse thoughts that keep me prisoner to things in my past or to worries about my future. My hope is in You. You are my strength and my shield. Transform my thoughts with the truth of Your Word. When I read the Bible, help me to remember Your Word. Then when my mind wanders to matters that bring me down, I will recall what You have to say about them.

✦ Cultivating a Good Attitude ✦

May the words of my mouth and the
meditation of my heart be pleasing to you,
O LORD, my rock and my redeemer.
PSALM 19:14 NLT

Lord, the Bible tells me life and death are in the power of the tongue. What comes out of my mouth is first planted in my mind as thoughts. Sometimes I say words I don't mean or later regret. Fill my spirit with Your goodness. Your words are healthy to me. Help me to control what I say by thinking about what pleases You before I open my mouth.

✦ Guarding My Mind ✦

Thank You for the helmet of salvation to protect my mind. As I spend time with You and in Your Word, I know I will become more like You. I will guard my mind and refuse to allow negative thoughts to have power over me. Your Word is my weapon to fight the thoughts that oppose who I am in Christ. I will be careful about the things I see and hear because I know they can open my mind to positive or negative thinking. Help me to focus on truth.

✦ Giving Something Completely to God ✦

People with their minds set on you,
you keep completely whole, steady on their feet,
because they keep at it and don't quit.
ISAIAH 26:3 MSG

When I pray, I give my concerns to You, but later I find that I've made them my responsibility again. Somewhere in my thinking I stop trusting You and try to work problems out on my own. I don't need to know how You are going to resolve them. Forgive me for making problems bigger than You, and show me how to give them completely to You.

⟶ An Attitude of Thankfulness ⟵

God, I appreciate the good things You put in my life. I know I take them for granted sometimes, and I don't mean to be that way. I get caught up with the fast-paced busyness of all the things I have to do. I need to remember the simple things that bring me joy: a moment of laughter, a smile from a stranger, and those moments when things are actually going right. I appreciate Your kindness and the fact that You made me Your child. Thank You!

⟶ To Be More Considerate ⟵

This you know, my beloved brethren.
But everyone must be quick to hear,
slow to speak and slow to anger.
JAMES 1:19 NASB

I could be more considerate. I admit it—I'm usually thinking of myself instead of someone else. Help me to be more considerate of others. Help me to listen when someone is speaking to me. Show me

what You want me to say when someone gives me
the opportunity to speak to them.

→ *Turning Obstacles into Opportunities* ←

Lord, You know I can get upset when things don't
go my way. I think a situation should play out a certain way and, when it doesn't, I lose focus and let
it ruin my whole day. Help me to see obstacles as
opportunities to maintain my composure. I want to
learn to rise above circumstances. Remind me that
in the light of eternity a few moments of inconve-
nience are not worth the effort and energy I waste
in negative emotional responses. Give me wisdom
to see life from Your perspective—sometimes my
way isn't the best way.

→ *An Attitude of Humility* ←

Lord, without You I am nothing. Sometimes I
want to rely on myself and do things my own way,
but I can't depend on my own morality and virtue. I need Your mercy and grace to become all
You created me to be. Help me to be content to
be myself. Remind me that I am as good as anyone else, but not better than anyone else. You love
equally—You love us all very much!

⮞ A Teachable Attitude ⮜

My son, pay attention to what I say;
turn your ear to my words. Do not let them out
of your sight, keep them within your heart;
for they are life to those who find them
and health to one's whole body.
PROVERBS 4:20–22 NIV

Holy Spirit, I invite You to be my teacher, to lead and guide me in all truth. Show me how to let go of selfish desires and listen to Your direction. I'll go where You want me to go today. Help me to focus my energy on Your instruction.

⮞ A Desire for Goodness ⮜

God, You are good, and I want to be good. You are like a rock; everything You do is perfect. You are always fair. You are my faithful God who does no wrong, who is right and fair. Let Your goodness drive my life. Help me to recognize sin and call it what it is—*sin*. No more excuses. I refuse to justify wrongdoing just because it's what I want. If it's wrong, it's not from You and I don't want it in my life. Give me a burning desire to hold on tightly to Your righteousness. In all I do, I want to please You.

✦ An Attitude of Mercy ✦

For the weapons of our warfare are not carnal
but mighty in God for pulling down strongholds,
casting down arguments and every high thing
that exalts itself against the knowledge of God,
bringing every thought into captivity
to the obedience of Christ.
2 CORINTHIANS 10:4–5 NKJV

Lord, when others treat me unfairly, judge me, or take something I feel I deserved, I want to get even. I want to fight for what is mine, but then I feel You urging me to show mercy. It's hard for me to do that.

✦ An Attitude of Repentance ✦

When I sin, I'm miserable. The weight of my sin puts pressure on my soul. It grips me and makes me feel that I deserve punishment—and I do! But You are always forgiving. Never let me take Your mercy lightly. I'm ashamed, and I don't want to come to You. Give me the courage to tell You the truth about all I've done. Help me always run *to* You—not away from You—when I fail. Then assure me of Your forgiveness and help me to forgive myself. Thank You for loving me, no matter what!

CHAPTER 17

My Responsibilities: The Power of Commitment

∞

Have you ever been disappointed when someone didn't follow through on a commitment they made to you? When someone you trust makes a promise to you, you normally build an expectation to see that promise through. Do you keep every promise you make? Are you responsible for your actions and words?

You can count on God to keep His promises and commitments. Our very world—the earth we walk, the air we breathe, and the water that sustains us—was created by His Word. God's Word holds everything together, and if the devil could get God to break His Word, just one time, all creation would cease to exist.

You are created in God's image, and your word has power. The more you protect your word and do what you say you will do, the more power your word has in your life and in the lives of those who trust you. Do you disappoint others with promises you can't keep? Excuses are just that—excuses. No matter how valid those excuses are, others will remember whether or not you followed through on your commitment.

You need people you can count on to keep their commitments, and your family and friends need to be able to count on you when you take on responsibility. They need to know you're going to deliver. And God needs to know that He can count on you, too.

Responsible people know the importance of counting the cost before they make a commitment that would make them responsible for the outcome. They count the cost.

The Book of Esther is a beautiful story of a young woman who counted the cost. She knew she could die if she approached the king without him first summoning her, but still she took action at the risk of her own life to save her people.

Jesus told us to count the cost before we build (Luke 14:28). Every day you build your life. You add to or take away from who you are becoming. Any responsibility you take on should be considered carefully before you commit to it. Ask yourself what it's going to cost if you do it, and what it's going to cost if you don't. There's always a cost— spiritually, emotionally, relationally, financially, and even physically.

Ask God to help you count the cost and, with His direction, commit to the things that will add to your life here on earth today and for all eternity.

✦ Accepting Responsibility for My Actions ✦

"Great gifts mean great responsibilities;
greater gifts, greater responsibilities!"
LUKE 12:48 MSG

It would be easier to deny my mistakes to myself
and to others, but I want to be a person of integrity
and honor. Truth is important to You—and to me.
Lord, give me the courage to take responsibility for
my actions. I know that with each action there are
consequences, both positive and negative. Help me
to think before I act and to listen to Your instruction and direction for decisions I make, no matter
how big or small.

✦ Accepting Responsibility for My Words ✦

My words are powerful—they can add to or take
away from someone's life. I want to be a positive
influence in the lives of those around me. I want
to encourage them with Your goodness and love. I
want to be truthful, and sometimes it's hard to say
certain things, but I'm asking You to help me speak
the truth in love. For those I have hurt with my
words, help me to take responsibility, apologize,
and set things right with them. Lord, put a guard
over my mouth so I speak Your words in love.

✦ Keeping Promises to Myself ✦

Each of you must take responsibility for doing the
creative best you can with your own life.
GALATIANS 6:5 MSG

Lord, You created me for a specific purpose. I make promises to myself and think it's okay not to keep them. Help me to remember that I'm responsible to You for how my life turns out. Help me to keep the commitments I've set and give me the courage to accomplish them. Remind me that it's okay to do good things for myself that help me to become the person You created me to be.

✦ Making Realistic Commitments ✦

Father, I want to live a balanced life. I am tired of people pulling at me. Show me how to choose what is important and necessary. Give me strength to say "no" when something doesn't belong on my list. I can't do everything that is asked of me. Help me to see what's important and when it's important. I want to remain stable in my spiritual, physical, emotional, relational, and financial needs. Teach me how to negotiate my time and energy—leaving plenty of time for rest and fun while doing what is necessary in all the other areas of my life.

⤖ *When I'm Tempted to Take Shortcuts* ⤛

*For we cannot oppose the truth,
but must always stand for the truth.*
2 CORINTHIANS 13:8 NLT

God, people around me take moral shortcuts, but I know that isn't right for me. You have given me values of honor, integrity, and truth. Help me not to compromise. Although others may act without integrity as they climb the corporate ladder, it's not worth the price of my relationship with You to follow their example. You bless me because I choose what is right and just. Thank You for reminding me of the way I need to go.

⤖ *When I'm Afraid to Commit* ⤛

I'm standing at a four-way stop. I don't know what to do. I have a huge decision in front of me but it means a high level of commitment. There's so much pressure to make a decision while I don't have all the facts. I'm conflicted and confused, but Your Word says that confusion is not of You. Help me to press through all the confusing clutter of this situation. Shine Your light on it and show me what You want me to do. Then if it's right, I'll do whatever it takes to be accountable, to see this thing through.

✣ When I Break a Promise ✣

Good people will be guided by honesty;
dishonesty will destroy those
who are not trustworthy.
PROVERBS 11:3 NCV

I did it again—I failed; I broke a promise. I feel guilty and ashamed. I thought I could pull it off, but I've hurt someone and disappointed myself and You. Forgive me for not counting the cost and thinking I could manage this alone. Give me the courage to apologize and correct my mistake, whatever it takes. Please comfort the people I hurt and help them to forgive me and maybe let me try again.

✣ Commitment to Prayer ✣

I get so busy with so many things that I often lose track of time and forget about You. Forgive me. I'm so sorry. I know You wait patiently for me to spend time with You. I'm asking You to remind me, prompt me, call to me. I promise to be more diligent with my time with You. You know everything there is to know about me. You hold all the answers for my life in the palm of Your hand. Help me to come to You, sit at Your feet, and listen carefully to the answers You have for my life questions.

✦ Keeping Commitments at Work ✦

Jesus, some people on my team are difficult to work with. Their ideas are different and their values are questionable, yet we have to succeed together. I have commitments to them that are hard to keep. Help me to represent You on the team. Show me how to fulfill my commitments by Your standards. Help me to serve my team members as You would serve them. Remind me that we succeed or fail only as a team.

✦ Keeping Commitments to Friends ✦

You yourself must be an example to them by doing good works of every kind. Let everything you do reflect the integrity and seriousness of your teaching. Teach the truth so your teaching can't be criticized. Then those who oppose us will be ashamed and have nothing bad to say about us.
TITUS 2:7–8 NLT

I don't mean to take advantage of others, but I've done it. Forgive me for it. Jesus, open my eyes to see that I hurt my friends when I'm late, cancel, or just don't show up. Let me see this before it's too late to keep my commitments. Teach me how to schedule for interruptions and still keep the appointments that are most important on the schedule.

❖ Enlisting the Help of Others ❖

Lord, why is it so hard sometimes to ask for help? I don't want people to think I'm weak or that the task is too hard. Change my perception of needing help. Give me a new understanding: asking for help doesn't mean I am weak, but that I value relationship with others. It says that I have confidence in their ability to assist me. Even when I need help from strangers, give me the courage to ask and to handle the rejection if they say "no." Grant me approval by those I ask for help.

❖ Counting the Cost ❖

*"For even if the mountains walk away
and the hills fall to pieces, My love won't walk
away from you, my covenant commitment of
peace won't fall apart." The GOD who
has compassion on you says so.*
ISAIAH 54:10 MSG

Everything I do or don't do costs me something—time, effort, emotional energy. When I choose, Lord, help me find balance. Will this added responsibility add to my life, add value to my relationships, or help me to achieve a higher standard of living at the cost of my health? Give me a reality check with each commitment I consider making.

✦ No More Excuses ✦

When I refuse to accept personal responsibility, I create my own problems. Lord, forgive me when I blame others for my situation instead of taking necessary steps to change my circumstances. Help me to accept my mistakes, look at them realistically, and learn from them. Help me find the courage in You to embrace my personal responsibility and see it as an opportunity to grow. Give me strength to make responsible choices. Guide me with Your wisdom in all I do, and help me see the truth of my actions clearly.

✦ God's Commitment to Me ✦

Remember his covenant forever—the commitment he made to a thousand generations.

Lord, You are great! I want the whole world to know what You have done for me. You have changed my life and set me free. I was lost and alone, and You found me. Everything I need is in You. You created me and crowned me with Your glory. You take responsibility for me, whether I succeed or fail. From the beginning of time, every promise You have made, You have kept. Generation after generation depends on You, just as I do.

1 CHRONICLES 16:15 NLT

CHAPTER 18

My Time: The Power of Priorities

It's important to be purposeful with your time. Every person on the planet has the same amount of time each day. You have to learn to manage yourself, because time refuses to be managed. (*Time* management is really *self* management—learning to use the inflexible twenty-four hours of the day in ways that best help you accomplish your goals.)

No one can change time, so you must continually remain aware of it. There are tools available to help you be more conscious of your time: clocks, watches, calendars, personal organizers, seminars, and computer programs. And still, we often find it difficult to make time to do everything we have to do.

Think of time as a currency—where do you spend it? Who or what will you give your time to today? Is that time wisely invested? You can probably think of many occasions when you let time get away from you. We've all looked up from a project or activity and realized we'd spent much more time on what we were doing than we intended.

Jesus said, "Wherever your treasure is, there

the desires of your heart will also be" (Matthew 6:21 NLT). So, how and where you choose to spend your time says a lot about what is most important to you.

The key to successful self-management is in setting priorities. Think back over the past few days or months. How did you spend your time, effort, and energy? Did you have a goal you were pushing to reach?

We need to allocate our time based on what we believe to be most important. Are our friends and family important? Then we schedule time for them. We *invest* our time in them.

As we read the Bible, it becomes clear that we are God's greatest priority. He has spent much of His time focused on bringing us back into relationship with Him.

Your relationship with God is the foundation of your success in everything else you do. All you will ever need is found in your relationship with Him. As you grow in Him, you become strong, healthy, and full of His love, and then you are able to overflow into the lives of others.

Through prayer and commitment to your relationship with God, He can help you make every minute count. He can help you focus on the things that are most important to you and to Him.

⇢ *The First Priority* ⇠

*" 'Love the Lord your God with all your heart
and with all your soul and with all your mind.'
This is the first and greatest commandment."*
MATTHEW 22:37–38 NIV

Father, You are my everything! Without You, I
wouldn't even be here. Forgive me for allowing
so many other things to squeeze between me and
You. Help me to become more diligent in my time
with You. It fills me with the strength I need to
make it day after day. I love You so much! I never
want to take our relationship for granted.

⇢ *Making Prayer a Priority* ⇠

God, I am reaching out to You from the deep-
est places in my heart. I love You and want to
make prayer a favorite part of my day. Help me
to be consistent in spending time with You. Teach
me to recognize and reject the distractions and the
unending list of things that keep me too busy for
You. My relationship with You is my highest priority and strongest commitment. Remind me of that
and give me the determination to spend time in
prayer no matter what situations arise. Let nothing
keep me from You!

❧ Living in the Now ❧

"And the second [greatest commandment] is like it:
'Love your neighbor as yourself.'"
MATTHEW 22:39 NIV

I can't change the past, but I think about it a lot. It's a waste of time, and I hate for my mind to go there. I don't want to recount my past mistakes—I've been forgiven. Lord, help me to focus on today. Help me to keep my attention on the priorities You have given me. Help me to live in the present. Show me what I can do today to make an eternal difference.

❧ Every Minute Counts ❧

What I do today affects my tomorrow. Lord, help me to be conscious of time wasters. I don't want to be idle and lazy. Show me Your plan and the things I need to put my hands to, but at the same time help me to balance my life so I take good care of my body and mind with the right amount of rest. As I walk with You, I know I am pursuing the things You want me to do. I ask You to help me be in the right place at the right time every time.

❖ When Others Fail Me ❖

Make allowance for each other's faults,
and forgive anyone who offends you.
Remember, the Lord forgave you,
so you must forgive others.
COLOSSIANS 3:13 NLT

When others fail me, it makes me feel unimportant to them. It hurts my feelings and I want to be angry. Remind me of the times when circumstances were out of my control and I missed a commitment and failed someone. Fill me with compassion and understanding for their situation. Help me to get over it and show them Your love.

❖ When I Make Excuses ❖

God, I know You aren't about excuses, but I make them when I don't want to do something I need to do. Forgive me for not being diligent. Give me strength to tackle the difficult tasks first, even those things I find boring. Help me to do the things I don't want to do as if I were doing them for You. That would give the job more purpose, at least for me. And remind me never to leave a job unfinished that I've committed to do. I want to leave a good impression on others, especially when I'm representing You.

➣ *When I'm Overcommitted* ➢

God, I did it again—I'm overcommitted, stressed, and overwhelmed. Someone I made a promise to is going to be disappointed in me. Why can't I just say "no" to start with? Help me to manage better and be realistic about what I can accomplish in one day. Give me wisdom when others ask me to help them. It's better to say "no" and help later, if I can, than to make a promise and then let someone down who was counting on me. When I make promises, help me to have the integrity to keep them.

➣ *Sacrifices* ➢

*You were taught to be made new in your hearts,
to become a new person. That new person is made
to be like God—made to be truly good and holy.*
EPHESIANS 4:23–24 NCV

I only have so much time every day. Lord, help me to spend my time wisely, on the things that matter most. Day-to-day things are continually in my face, screaming for my attention, but there are also things that are eternal, like people. Help me realize my time spent for eternal things, like spending time with others, is not a sacrifice, but a reward.

❖ When I'm Distracted ❖

Lord, my mind is wandering again. Help me to stay focused on what I have in front of me. I have the mind of Christ and I am determined to stay steady until I've finished the task. I will not look to the right or the left. I refuse to be distracted. I push my worries to the side. I will accomplish what I've set my heart to do. I will not quit. I have a mission and I will achieve it.

❖ Getting the Most Out of My Day ❖

But most of all, my brothers and sisters,
never take an oath, by heaven or earth
or anything else. Just say a simple yes or no,
so you will not sin and be condemned.
JAMES 5:12 NLT

Father, when I was a child a day seemed so long that sometimes I got bored. Now, I find there are not enough hours to complete what I need to do each day. I need Your wisdom about how to budget my time. Show me how I can use it more efficiently.

✦ Enjoying Time Alone ✦

God, sometimes I feel guilty when I make time to be alone. My relationships are important to me, but time alone is important, too. Jesus took time to get away and be alone. Teach me to follow His example. Remind me to spend that time reflecting on the many good things You have done in my life. Remembering those times helps me to grow stronger in my faith. Time alone is a great opportunity to study Your Word and let You minister to me. Help me to enjoy my alone time with You.

✦ Tools for Time ✦

Instruct them to do good, to be rich in good works,
to be generous and ready to share, storing up
for themselves the treasure of a good foundation
for the future, so they may take hold
of that which is life indeed.
1 TIMOTHY 6:18–19 NASB

Lord, help me to find tools to make me more effective in the use of my time. Bring the right people across my path to educate me about how to use the tools that best fit my personality and gifts.

❖ Knowing What's Important ❖

With each passing day, I'm facing new demands on my time and energy. Father, help me to know what is most important. I know that growing in my relationship with You is first, so I need Your help in staying true to that commitment. Second, I need Your help in valuing the relationships You bring into my life and caring for them with the power of Your love. Please tap me on the shoulder and remind me when I'm becoming too busy. I don't want to miss the most important priorities in life.

❖ The Right Time ❖

People can make all kinds of plans,
but only the LORD's plan will happen.
PROVERBS 19:21 NCV

Father, I have lots of ideas. There's so much I want to do, but I just don't know when to do it. Your timing is everything. You have ordered my steps and You know the way that I should go. I ask the Holy Spirit to lead and guide me. Give me assurance and peace to know when it's time to step forward. Thank You for making everything happen in Your time, not mine.

CHAPTER 19

My Dreams: The Power of Expectation

∞

Steve Jobs, CEO for Apple, Inc., said, "The people who are crazy enough to think they can change the world are the ones who do." If you think about it, his words are true. Consider all the people who attempted something they were told they never could do, but succeeded. Now, that success may have come only after many failures at trying to achieve that dream.

The most important thing to realize is whether or not the dream is God-given. When our dreams line up with God's will for our lives, then we can trust Him to meet our expectations. God's ways are higher than our ways, and sometimes we have to let His plan play out without interfering. It helps not to hold so tightly to what you've imagined it to be, but instead remain open to the way God wants to do it. Sometimes the way we want to go isn't the same road God wants us to take. Ephesians 3:20 says God "is able to do exceeding abundantly above all that we ask or think." What if our asking and thinking fall short of what we are able to do or become? The power to achieve your goals and dreams isn't in the dream itself but in the expectation that God is faithful to make it happen!

Another reason we miss the goal that God has for our lives is because we quit. "Let us not become weary in doing good, for at the proper time we will reap a harvest if we do not give up" (Galatians 6:9 NIV). There will always be opposition to our faith, challenging us and questioning if we *truly* believe. We have to hold fast to the promises of God and trust Him to carry us through.

It takes prayer and commitment to see God's plan for your life revealed. God lives beyond your expectations—the more you trust Him for His very best, the higher you can go. What would happen in your life today if you *really* let go and let God take you where He desires you to go? When you continue to press forward with the expectation that He'll see you through, His dreams for your life can become reality.

⇢ *The Power to Believe* ⇠

Father, I have many dreams, but I've also experienced disappointment. I want to believe I can achieve my dreams. When I'm discouraged, help me to remember that all things are possible when I believe. I know Your expectations for my life are greater than I can imagine. Bring me back to Your promises when I'm tempted to think I can't achieve, because Your Word says I can do all things through Christ who gives me strength. I draw on that strength now for courage to push forward.

✣ Christ's Return ✣

"You also must be ready all the time, for the Son of Man will come when least expected."
LUKE 12:40 NLT

Lord, forgive me. I say I'm a Christian and that I believe in You, but my focus is so much on today that I don't live like I expect You to return at any moment. You should be my focus, and Your return is what I should look forward to. Remind me of the eternal. Help me to remember that this world is not my home and that my journey is just beginning with You.

✣ High Expectations ✣

My high expectations can leave me disappointed. Sometimes I'm disappointed because I imagine how You're going to work everything out for me, yet the outcome doesn't look like I thought it would. I'm afraid all I've hoped for won't happen. But then You outdo Yourself and it's better than I could ever imagine. Forgive me for my doubt. Remind me of

Your faithfulness. Help me to trust You from the time I pray to the time I receive Your answer.

⤖ Unmet Expectations ⤖

*Let us hold tightly without wavering
to the hope we affirm, for God can
be trusted to keep his promise.*
HEBREWS 10:23 NLT

Lord, my expectations were high, and I'm so disappointed in what looks to be the outcome of this situation. Help me to remember that You are in control. I've given this situation to You. Help me to let go of it once again. You are faithful and just, and You always deliver what You promise. It doesn't look like what I expected, but I'm learning that Your way is always better in the end.

⤖ To Dream Again ⤖

Lord, You know all the big dreams I once had for the future. I don't want to admit it, but I've given up on my dreams. They seemed so impossible, and my desire to see them through slowly faded away. I want to dream again. I want to experience the future You planned for me. Give me a red-hot fire for my dream that won't go out. Show me those people who will support my endeavors and please shield me from those who won't. Give me Your supernatural grace, peace, and endurance to achieve my dream.

✣ *Pursuing My Dream* ✣

I press toward the goal for the prize of the upward call of God in Christ Jesus.
PHILIPPIANS 3:14 NKJV

You gave me a gift and I want to use it to begin the work You have for me to do. Your only Son, Jesus, knew His mission while on the earth, and He completed it. Father, give me the drive, power, and determination to accomplish my mission. I am committed and ready to pursue my dream. Thank You for the courage to move forward. I am stepping out in faith today.

✣ *Getting Back on Track* ✣

Lord, I fully believe I was born with God-given purpose, but I feel like my life is going nowhere. There's got to be more! I feel displaced, like I stepped off Your road map for my life. There's a fire burning within me to get back on track. Help me to remove the distractions and focus on You.

I want to hear Your voice and go where You are leading me. I'm begging You, intervene in my life today. I'm willing and committed to doing what You tell me to do. Help me find my place.

☙ When I'm Tired ❧

God, I've been pushing myself so hard lately. I need some downtime. I don't want to grow weary and quit, but I need some breathing room. Help me to take time to rest and relax. It seems I've faced so many obstacles in pursuit of my dreams. I know I can do it. Refresh me today with Your presence. Fill me with Your peace and restore me in Your love. As soon as I gain the strength to press on, I'll take another breath and dive in, pressing hard to reach my goals again.

☙ To See It Through ❧

The way of the good person is like the light of dawn, growing brighter and brighter until full daylight.
PROVERBS 4:18 NCV

I've imagined my life in different ways, but it isn't turning out as I thought it would. I've found rough waters at every turn. You never said it would be easy, but You have promised to do exceedingly more than I can imagine. Help me to see this dream through to reality. Show me what it looks like from Your perspective. Help me not to fall short, but to rise to the level You desire me to reach.

✢ Sharing My Dream with Others ✦

Father, sometimes I get disappointed when I share my dream with others. People can be negative, and hearing their lack of enthusiasm over and over discourages me. I need people who will be excited about my plans. Give me wisdom in who I share my dream with. Teach me how to overcome negativity. Please show me Your words of wisdom that will build me up in faith. Bring supporters who will cheer me on as I race for the prize of accomplishment. And more than anything, remind me that my confidence is in You.

✢ When I Drag My Feet ✦

Lazy people want much but get little,
but those who work hard will prosper.
PROVERBS 13:4 NLT

Why am I procrastinating in moving forward? Is that me or You? Speak to my heart, Lord. What is set before me seems hard. And maybe I'm a little afraid, but You are with me. I don't want to miss anything You have prepared for me, but I'm willing to wait for Your leading. I need to know Your timing on this. Give me wisdom and tell me when to jump in.

✦ Commitment to God's Dream ✦

Lord, I'm ready to make a commitment to work with You to fulfill the plan You have for my life. All that You have asked of me, I will do. Thank You that I don't have to do anything alone. You are always here with me. You make the resources I need available to me to get the job done. I'm trusting You to give me strength when I jump the hurdles before me. No matter what I need, You have the answer. I commit my work to You, Lord. I trust You to establish it and set me firmly on a foundation of faith.

✦ Removing the Limits ✦

Listen to my voice in the morning, LORD.
Each morning I bring my requests
to you and wait expectantly.
PSALM 5:3 NLT

Father, You have promised to hear me when I pray and to honor me as I serve You. We're doing this together. I am removing the limits that have constrained me in the past. It doesn't matter what other people think; my heart is tuned to Your voice. I hear Your words, and I determine never to follow a discouraging voice. Nothing is impossible with You.

⤳ *Patience for the Dream* ⤆

God, I want to see results quickly, but I understand that's not realistic. I need to give You time to work behind the scenes. It would be so much easier to wait if I knew the details from Your perspective, but that's not faith. Forgive me when I want to take control, or when I try to make things happen on my own timeline. Help me to stand strong, believing that the final outcome is exactly what You want it to be. I trust You, knowing You will get us to our dream.

Chapter 20

My World: The Power of Compassion

∞

Therefore, as God's chosen people, holy and dearly loved, clothe yourselves with compassion, kindness, humility, gentleness and patience.

Colossians 3:12 niv

Compassion is defined by *Merriam-Webster Dictionary* as "sympathetic consciousness of others' distress together with a desire to alleviate it." Our God is the Father of compassion. He had so much sympathy for our suffering that He sent His one and only Son to die for us (see John 3:16). We, God's people, are to be clothed with compassion (see Colossians 3:12). What are you wearing today?

Some of us, when our tender hearts see the troubles of others, may think we are too far away or too powerless to help. But that is an untruth. Our prayers are full of heavenly power. They transcend time and space. We can be on our knees in our living rooms and reach a president in the White House, a homeless man on a city street, children starving in North Korea, missionaries in South America, or an AIDS worker in Africa. With the power of compassion combined with prayer, *we can make a difference!*

Nehemiah was an unselfish man of prayer who looked beyond himself and his needs. His example shows us what we need to do to be powerful intercessors for this world. Like Nehemiah, we need to find out what is happening outside the sphere of me, myself, and I. When Nehemiah met Hanani, one of his brothers who had come from Judah, Nehemiah *asked for news* of the Jews in Jerusalem. It was then that he found out the specifics of the remnant's desperate situation, how the wall of Jerusalem was broken down, leaving the Jews defenseless against their enemies (see Nehemiah 1:1–3).

As soon as he heard of their situation, Nehemiah sat down and wept. *He felt compassion* and his heart mourned. The Bible says he fasted and *prayed,* asking God to hear him, remember His promises to His people, and give him success (see Nehemiah 1:4–11).

A few months later Nehemiah took wine to King Artaxerxes, and with one look at his cupbearer's face, which revealed "sadness of heart," the king inquired as to Nehemiah's troubles, asking what he could do for him. Here Nehemiah *took direct action* as he reached out to another. Through that assistance, he was able to personally assess the situation in Jerusalem and, ultimately, to help rebuild the wall.

Nehemiah was *filled with faith*, telling those who later ridiculed the rebuilding, " 'The God of heaven will give us success' " (Nehemiah 2:20 NIV).

What walls can you help rebuild? What needs do you see outside of yourself? For what areas—your church, your school, your government—is God prompting you to pray? To what dire situations—world hunger, terrorism, war, crime—is your heart drawn?

When you hear of distress in the world and your heart responds with compassion, make a difference! Get down on your knees and pray with persistence. And if so led, take direct action. Be filled with confidence that God will work in the situation.

In this world, Jesus says we will have trouble. When things seem hopeless, we must be confident that Christ will meet us in the fire, as He did Shadrach, Meshach, and Abednego. When terror seems to reign on every side, continue faithfully onward, remembering that "if we are thrown into the blazing furnace, the God we serve is able to deliver us from it, and he will deliver us" (Daniel 3:17 NIV). Because of His unfailing compassion, we will not be consumed (see Lamentations 3:22).

✢ Praise for the Father of Compassion ✢

Blessed be the God and Father
of our Lord Jesus Christ, the Father
of mercies and God of all comfort.
2 CORINTHIANS 1:3 NKJV

Lord, You love us so much. Fill me with that love to overflowing. Give me a compassionate heart. Lead me to the concern You would like me to champion for You, whether it be working in a soup kitchen, helping the homeless, or adopting a missionary couple. Lead me in prayer as I go down on my knees and intercede for others in distress.

✢ Intercession for World Leaders ✢

First of all, then, I urge that entreaties and prayers,
petitions and thanksgivings, be made on
behalf of all men, for kings and all who
are in authority, so that we may lead a tranquil
and quiet life in all godliness and dignity.
1 TIMOTHY 2:1–2 NASB

Dear God, today I lift up the world leaders— presidents, premiers, kings, queens, prime ministers, ambassadors to the United Nations, all rulers, princes, and governors. Give them wisdom, give them courage, give them minds of peace. There is so much death and destruction in this world and at times I feel disheartened. But I know where to turn—to You, my Father, who makes all things right.

✦ Perseverance in Prayer ✦

As you know, we count as blessed those who have persevered. You have heard of Job's perseverance and have seen what the Lord finally brought about. The Lord is full of compassion and mercy.
JAMES 5:11 NIV

I feel like I've been praying forever for a situation that does not seem to be changing, Lord. I feel like Job: Here I am on my knees in prayer while the entire world dissolves around me. But I know that You are in control. You know all things. So once again, I lift my concern up to You, confident that You will handle the situation in Your timing.

✦ God's Hand Guarding Us ✦

*I pray not that thou shouldest take them out of the
world, but that thou shouldest keep them from the evil.
They are not of the world, even as I am not of
the world. . . . As thou hast sent me into the world,
even so have I also sent them into the world.*
JOHN 17:15–16, 18

Lord, sometimes I feel like Captain Kirk. When
faced with the evils of this world, I want to say,
"Beam me up, God!" But I know that no matter
what happens in this world, Your hand is
guarding us. And armed with Your compassion,
we have the power to intercede for the hungry,
the oppressed, the imprisoned, the homeless, the
wounded.

✦ Reigning Peace ✦

*[Jesus said,] These things I have spoken
unto you, that in me ye might have peace.
In the world ye shall have tribulation:
but be of good cheer; I have overcome the world.*
JOHN 16:33

Dear God, how I pray for peace around the world.
Some say it's impossible—but with You all things
are possible. And while peace may not yet reign

throughout the earth, with You in my heart, peace reigns within, for You have overcome the world! May all people feel Your peace within!

⊹ Compassion for the Hungry ⊱

Is there any encouragement from belonging to Christ? Any comfort from his love? Any fellowship together in the Spirit? Are your hearts tender and compassionate? Then make me truly happy by agreeing wholeheartedly with each other, loving one another, and working together with one mind and purpose.
PHILIPPIANS 2:1–2 NLT

With the compassion You show to us, Your abiding tenderness through thick and thin, today I reach out to the hungry here and abroad. Open up my eyes to how I can help. Show me where my hands can be used to help feed those who are starving. I want to serve others in the name of Jesus Christ, for that is what You have called us to do. Open a door for me. Show me what I can do to make this world a better place.

☙ Community Peace and Understanding ❧

*The weapons we fight with are not the weapons
of the world. On the contrary, they have
divine power to demolish strongholds.*

2 CORINTHIANS 10:4 NIV

God, through the divine power of Your Spirit and
Your Word, I pray for my neighborhood. Demolish the strongholds of evil within this community.
Touch each heart with Your peace and understanding. You know what each family needs. Help me to
be an encouragement to them. Be with me as I take
a prayer walk around this neighborhood, lifting each
family up to Your heavenly throne.

☙ Comfort for the Suffering ❧

*[Jesus said,] "You are the light of the world—like
a city on a hilltop that cannot be hidden."*

MATTHEW 5:14 NLT

Dearest Christ, I pray for Your bright, shining light to
spread out into the world. For Your love to reach the
ends of the earth. Give comfort to those who suffer
from abuse and violence. Touch them with Your healing light and guard them with Your protective hand.
Give them assurance that You are there. Allow them
to feel Your presence, hear Your voice, feel Your touch.

✦ Change the Hearts of Terrorists ✦

Finally, all of you, be like-minded, be sympathetic,
love one another, be compassionate and humble.
1 PETER 3:8 NIV

Dear Lord, please soften the calloused hearts of those who deem themselves terrorists. Exchange their hearts of stone for ones tender with love. Protect the innocent here and abroad, especially missionaries who risk their lives to spread Your light. Comfort those who have lost loved ones through the violence around the world. Lord, can't we all just get along?

✦ Victory for Youth ✦

For our struggle is not against flesh and blood,
but against the rulers, against the powers,
against the world forces of this darkness,
against the spiritual forces of wickedness
in the heavenly places.
EPHESIANS 6:12 NASB

Lord, I pray that You would oust the unseen evils from this land, that Your angels would battle fiercely against the dark forces corrupting our youth. Empower our youth leaders to claim a victory for young hearts. Show me how I can help at my church, how I can lead teens to You. Give parents the right words to say when dealing with their children.

✦ Protection for Missionaries and Pastors ✦

"If it be so, our God whom we serve is able to deliver us from the furnace of blazing fire; and He will deliver us."
DANIEL 3:17 NASB

I pray for others with the confidence that You, dear Lord, hear my prayer. That although at times this world seems so unsettled, Your hand is upon our missionaries and pastors, guarding them when they are awake and as they sleep. Give them the strength to do what You have called them to do. Give them the means to help the lost, starving, diseased, and imprisoned. Give them wisdom as they reveal Your Word and reach into the darkness to spread Your light.

✦ Message of Eternal Life ✦

The world and its desires pass away, but whoever does the will of God lives forever.
1 JOHN 2:17 NIV

The world may pass away, but Your love never

fails. Those who believe in You will live with You forever. What a blessed thing! I pray that others around the world will hear the message so that they, too, can accept Your gift of eternal life. Show me how I can help spread the message, all to Your glory.

✦ Clothed with Compassion ✦

Therefore, as God's chosen people,
holy and dearly loved, clothe yourselves
with compassion, kindness, humility,
gentleness and patience.
COLOSSIANS 3:12 NIV

As I get down on my knees, I wrap myself within the cloak of compassion. I bring to You specific concerns for which You have led me to pray, knowing that You hear my prayer, confident that You will answer. And as I rise from the place of prayer, may Your kindness, humility, gentleness, and patience shine through me and lighten the hearts of others. I want to be Your servant. Help me to change the world.

❧ Home, School, and Streets ❧

You are of God, little children,
and have overcome them, because He who is
in you is greater than he who is in the world.

1 JOHN 4:4 NKJV

Lord, there are so many dark forces within our schools, on the streets, and even in our homes. I pray for Your light to eliminate the evil among us. I know that no matter what, You will prevail, dear Jesus. You have overcome this world. You have the power to do the impossible. Show me how I can make this world a better place. Give me the heart to intercede for others and the courage to step in when and where I am needed.

CHAPTER 21

My Challenges: The Power of Faith-Based Boldness

∞

When we trust in him, we're free
to say whatever needs to be said,
bold to go wherever we need to go.
EPHESIANS 3:11 MSG

Remember the Star Trek series? At the beginning of every episode, we'd hear Captain Kirk's voice saying, "Space, the final frontier. These are the voyages of the starship *Enterprise*. Its five-year mission: To explore strange new worlds. To seek out new life and new civilizations. To boldly go where no man has gone before."

Okay, so we're not starships, but we are stars in God's eyes. And since each of our lives is uniquely different, we often encounter situations where "no man has gone before." But how can we learn to face each new "enterprise" boldly? We can start by modeling the kind of faith-based boldness that David exhibited during his encounter with Goliath (see 1 Samuel 17).

The youngest of Jesse's sons, David spent many hours in the fields, taking care of his father's sheep.

It was here that David prayed and meditated on God, his constant companion. His reliance on God to deliver him from lions and bears in the wild was evidence of the intimate relationship David had developed with God at an early age. This intimacy with the Lord allowed David's faith to grow. David knew God would be with him in every situation. It was his faith that gave him the boldness to do whatever God called him to do.

When David left his father's fields to check on his brothers who were with King Saul's army, it was not by chance that his visit coincided with the nine-foot-nine-inch-tall Philistine warrior named Goliath, who was defying the army of Israel. As David began talking to the soldiers, he encountered his first challenge in the form of his oldest brother, Eliab, who said, "Why have you come down? And with whom have you left those few sheep in the wilderness? I know your insolence and the wickedness of your heart; for you have come down in order to see the battle" (1 Samuel 17:28 NASB).

Now David *could* have taken this attack upon his character to heart. But because of his faith-based boldness, David did not allow Eliab's negative comments to take root in his mind. He was able to simply turn away and continue on his mission.

David's next confrontation was with King Saul, who "from his shoulders upward. . .was taller than any of the [other children of Israel]"

(1 Samuel 9:2 NKJV). Now, you'd think that because of his size Saul himself would have fought Goliath. Instead, Saul tried to discourage the only one willing to face the giant. Saul said to David: "There's no way you can fight this Philistine and possibly win! You're only a boy, and he's been a man of war since his youth" (1 Samuel 17:33 NLT).

Saul was right. Although David had always managed to keep his lambs safe, he had no battlefield experience. But inexperience can be a good thing. David had always relied on God to deliver him and he wasn't about to stop doing so now—nor was he going to allow Saul to dampen his enthusiasm. Instead, he boldly responded to his king: "I've been a shepherd, tending sheep for my father. Whenever a lion or bear came and took a lamb from the flock, I'd go after it, knock it down, and rescue the lamb. If it turned on me, I'd grab it by the throat, wring its neck, and kill it. Lion or bear, it made no difference—I killed it. And I'll do the same to this Philistine pig who is taunting the troops of God-Alive. GOD, who delivered me from the teeth of the lion and the claws of the bear, will deliver me from this Philistine" (1 Samuel 17:34–37 MSG).

Our David was so successful in refuting Saul's discouraging remarks that the king himself became enthusiastic and said to him, "Go! And may God help you."

When David eventually drew near the Philistines, dressed not in Saul's bulky chain mail, helmet, and sword but in shepherd's garb, and armed with only five stones and a sling, his appearance revealed that his confidence was in God and God alone.

Goliath took one look at this lowly shepherd boy and began to taunt him. David responded to such intimidation by declaring that he came in the name of God, that he depended upon God for success, and that this success would all be to God's glory! Then David actually "*hurried and ran* toward the army to meet the Philistine" (1 Samuel 17:48 NKJV, emphasis added). What boldness!

Unlike Saul and Eliab, David was able "to boldly go where no man has gone before." Because of his intimate knowledge of God, David was able to turn away from a maligner, defend himself before a discourager, and fell a giant intimidator with one smooth stone. By using faith-based boldness, David meet the challenges presented to him and, as a result, routed the entire Philistine army. All for God's glory!

If we build up our confidence by spending time in the Word, prayer, and meditation, getting to know our God intimately, we can be like David, who, with faith-based boldness, "rose early in the morning" (1 Samuel 17:20 NKJV) to meet every challenge God put in his path.

⇥ *Dissuaded from Your Goal* ⇤

*They were just trying to intimidate us,
imagining that they could discourage us and
stop the work. So I continued the work
with even greater determination.*
NEHEMIAH 6:9 NLT

Lord, here I am trying to take on this work and others are trying to intimidate me, telling me there is no way I can meet the challenge You have set before me. But I have faith in You. I know that with You in my life, I can do whatever You call me to do. Help me not to let others dissuade me from my goal. Give me the faith that David sought from You, the kind that does not waver but goes boldly forward.

⇥ *Bold and Diligent* ⇤

*"Be bold and diligent.
And GOD be with you as you do your best."*
2 CHRONICLES 19:11 MSG

I'm working as hard as I can to meet my challenge. I want to do my best, knowing that You are with me all the way. Help me to be brave. Help me not to panic. Neither fear nor anxiety is of You. I need to focus on You, to build up my faith and my confidence. Help me not to deviate from my course. I am here this morning, ready to listen to Your voice. Lead me, gentle Shepherd, where You want me to go.

⤖ Facing the Unknown ⤆

"And now, compelled by the Spirit, I am going to Jerusalem, not knowing what will happen to me there."
ACTS 20:22 NIV

O Lord, I feel called to take on this new challenge. I can feel the Spirit drawing me into this latest endeavor. But I don't know what's going to happen. Oh, how I sometimes wish I could see into the future. Lord, help me to have confidence, trust, and faith in Your will for my life. Help me to just put one foot in front of the other, to do the next thing, to continue walking in Your way. And when I get there, I will give You all the glory!

⤖ Fearlessness ⤆

*Though an army may encamp against me,
my heart shall not fear.*
PSALM 27:3 NKJV

I remember the story of David, how he faced opposition from his brother, his king, and then a huge giant, all under the watchful eye of his enemies. But he was not afraid. Oh, that I would have such faith. Sometimes I get so scared my heart begins beating a mile a minute. And those are the times when I have taken my eyes off of You. Keep my focus on Your Word. Plant this verse in my heart so that when dread comes upon me, I can say these words and kiss fear good-bye.

→ Standing with God ←

Everyone deserted me. May it not be held against them. But the Lord stood at my side and gave me strength. . . . And I was delivered.
2 TIMOTHY 4:16–17 NIV

All of a sudden, I am as alone as David when he stood before Goliath. But I am not going to be mad at others for deserting me. I don't need them. All I need is You. You are my Lord, my Savior, my Deliverer, my Rock, my Refuge. You are by my side. I can feel Your presence right here, right now. Oh, how wonderful You are! Thank You for giving me the power I need. Thank You for never leaving me.

✦ Support of Fellow Believers ✦

*When [Paul] would not be dissuaded, we gave up
and said, "The Lord's will be done."*
ACTS 21:14 NIV

Sometimes those who don't know You think that
believers like me are crazy. But we're not. We just
know that when You call us to do something, when
You put a challenge before us, we are to go forward with no fear. We are bold in You, Lord! How
awesome is that! And thankfully, fellow believers
encourage us, knowing that if it is Your will, all will
be well. What would I do without that support?
Thank You for planting my feet in a nice broad
place, surrounded by fellow believers who love and
pray for me.

✦ Our Help ✦

*Our help is in the name of the LORD,
who made heaven and earth.*
PSALM 124:8 NKJV

I need look no further than You, Lord, to help me.
It is Your name that I trust. It is Your power that
will help me meet this challenge. After all, You
made heaven and earth. You made me. You know
the plan for my life. You have equipped me to do

what You have called me to do. Help me not to rely on myself but on You and Your power. That is what is going to give me victory in this life. Thank You for hearing and answering my prayer.

→ My Armor ←

I will not trust in my bow, nor shall my sword
save me. But You have saved us from our enemies,
and have put to shame those who hated us.
In God we boast all day long,
and praise Your name forever.
PSALM 44:6–8 NKJV

I do not trust in my talents, diligence, money, education, luck, or others to help me meet this challenge. I trust in You. My power is in the faith-based boldness that only comes from knowing You intimately. With that weapon in my arsenal, there is only victory ahead. Those who say I cannot do what You have called me to do will be put to shame. But that's not why I continue to meet this challenge. I go forward because I want to bring glory to you. It is in You that I boast all day long. I praise Your name, my Strength and my Deliverer.

✦ Hope ✦

"And now, Lord, what do I wait for?
My hope is in You."
Psalm 39:7 nkjv

Some hope in employers or money or connections or that one big break. I hope in You and what You want to do through me while I'm here on earth. Don't let me drag my feet in fear but boldly run forward as David did when he faced Goliath. David knew You, and he knew that You would always be with him, no matter what. That's a fabulous faith. That's faith-based boldness! Empower me with that today so that I, like David, can go out with You and take on giants.

✦ Make Me Bold ✦

On the day I called, You answered me;
You made me bold with strength in my soul.
Psalm 138:3 nasb

Sometimes I feel like a ninety-five-pound weakling when it comes to my faith. I let my doubts and fears overtake me and then find myself shrinking from the challenges You put before me. Lord, I ask You to make me bold. Give me the strength to take on all comers. To do what You want me to do.

Dispel the darkness that surrounds me. Warm me with the light of Your face. Bring me to where You want to be. Give me strength in my soul!

⤚ By Faith, I Go ⤙

By faith Abraham, when he was called,
obeyed by going out to a place which he was
to receive for an inheritance; and he went out,
not knowing where he was going.
HEBREWS 11:8 NASB

In these days of online direction services and personal navigation systems, I can't imagine not knowing where I am going. What Abraham might have given for a map! But that's what faith is all about, isn't it? It's the substance of things hoped for, the evidence of things unseen (see Hebrews 11:1). So give me that faith, Lord, as I take on this challenge. I don't know where it will lead or how it will all turn out, but by faith I will obey this call You have put upon my life. I will go out, not knowing, because I trust in You!

✢ At the Throne ✦

So let us come boldly to the throne of our gracious God.
There we will receive his mercy, and we will
find grace to help us when we need it most.
HEBREWS 4:16 NLT

Here I am again, Lord, coming boldly before You, kneeling at the foot of Your throne. I need Your mercy this morning, and although it seems like I ask for this over and over again, give me more faith, Lord. Help me not to run from this challenge. Give me the grace, strength, energy, talent, and intelligence that I need to make this come out right. I come to You, bowing down, asking for Your love and power to fill me and give me the strength I need to accomplish the challenges before me this day.

✢ God Looks at the Heart ✦

But the LORD said to Samuel, "Do not consider
his appearance or his height, for I have rejected him.
The LORD does not look at the things people look at.
People look at the outward appearance,
but the LORD looks at the heart."
1 SAMUEL 16:7 NIV

Some people look at me and say, "There's no way you can do this." But with You I can do anything,

Lord. You don't just look at my appearance. When You look at me, You look directly at my heart. I know that You have made me to use my particular talents to accomplish particular tasks here on earth. You know my purpose, my path. Help me use all my resources to meet this challenge before me. All to Your glory!

✦ *In God's Strength* ✦

I have strength for all things in Christ Who empowers me [I am ready for anything and equal to anything through Him Who infuses inner strength into me; I am self-sufficient in Christ's sufficiency].
PHILIPPIANS 4:13 AMP

It's amazing—I can do all things through You! You give me the power! You give me the energy! You give me the ways and the means! As I lie here, in Your presence, I feel all the energy emanating from You. Oh, what a feeling! Give me that strength I need to accomplish the goals You set before me. Plant the words, "I can do all things through God—He strengthens me!" in my heart forever and ever.

Conclusion

∞

I hope that you have enjoyed these chapters and have benefited in your faith life. Since we are redeemed by grace alone through faith alone, it is essential that we learn how to strengthen our faith in every area of our walk with God.

As I began writing this conclusion, the mail was delivered to my home and in it was a card from a sweet older lady in my church. In it she wrote simply, "Our faith may be tested so that we may trust His faithfulness." What wonderful timing! I think she is on to something. God's faithfulness can't grow to be any better or stronger than it is right now. It is our faith that needs strengthening, and it is through the challenges of daily living that this growth occurs.

The same faith that secures our eternity with God is the faith that enables us to trust God for the smaller things. The health of our finances, our relationships, our church life, and our roles depends on the level of faith we have in God. So let us come boldly to His throne and ask for the grace that we need to have the type of faith He requires.

*We remember before our God and Father
your work produced by faith,
your labor prompted by love,
and your endurance inspired by
hope in our Lord Jesus Christ.*

1 Thessalonians 1:3 niv

Notes

_____

_____

_____

_____

_____

_____

_____

_____

_____

_____

_____

Notes

_____

_____

_____

_____

_____

_____

_____

_____

_____

_____

_____

Notes

_____

_____

_____

_____

_____

_____

_____

_____

_____

_____

_____

_____